America's Best-Loved
Community Cookbook Recipes

Family Dinners

Better Homes and Gardens®

Better Homes and Gardens® Books
Des Moines

Better Homes and Gardens® Books
An Imprint of Meredith® Books

America's Best-Loved Community Cookbook Recipes
Family Dinners
Editor: Christopher Cavanaugh
Associate Art Director: Lynda Haupert
Designer: Jeff Harrison
Copywriter: Kim Gayton Elliott
Copy Editor: Kathy Roberts
Production Manager: Doug Johnston

Editor-in-Chief: James D. Blume
Director, New Product Development: Ray Wolf
Test Kitchen Director: Sharon Stilwell

Better Homes and Gardens® **Magazine**
Editor-in-Chief: Jean LemMon
Executive Food Editor: Nancy Byal

Meredith Publishing Group
President, Publishing Group: Christopher M. Little
Vice President and Publishing Director: John P. Loughlin

Meredith Corporation
Chairman and Chief Executive Officer: Jack D. Rehm
President and Chief Operating Officer: William T. Kerr

Chairman of the Executive Committee: E.T. Meredith III

On the cover: Buttermilk Fried Chicken and Biscuits (see recipe, page 18)

Our seal assures you that every recipe in **America's Best-Loved Community Cookbook Recipes:** *Family Dinners* has been tested in the Better Homes and Gardens® Test Kitchen. This means that each recipe is practical and reliable, and meets our high standards of taste appeal. We guarantee your satisfaction with this book for as long as you own it.

family dinners

For many, "dinner time" has come to mean "family time"—when everyone gathers together to eat and share stories of school and work. In this volume of *America's Best-Loved Community Cookbook Recipes,* Better Homes and Gardens® is pleased to offer a marvelous assortment of meals for every day of the week—and few things will get your family to the table faster and encourage them to stay longer than these delectable dinners.

Need a comfort-food supper for a cold winter evening? Buttermilk Fried Chicken and Biscuits or Swiss Bliss will banish the chill and satisfy the hungriest soul without fail. Want to treat your family to a feast alfresco? Barbecue Butterflied Leg of Lamb or Blackened Redfish are both fine warm-weather fare. In *Family Dinners* you'll find recipes to tempt any palate and dishes to serve any season for any culinary need. And because each and every recipe has earned the Better Homes and Gardens® Test Kitchen seal of approval, you can be confident that every dish you make will be a sure-fire success with your family.

Tips from our kitchen, serving suggestions, savvy substitutions, and more are included to add to your cooking and eating pleasure. And, as always in *America's Best-Loved Community Cookbook Recipes,* you'll find the amusing, touching, intriguing, and heartwarming human story behind each of these *Family Dinners.*

contents

poultry

Let your family feast on any one of these prized poultry recipes and you'll hear raves about dinner for weeks to come. For a down-home scrumptious supper, serve Honey Lime Chicken, Turkey Loaf, or Roast Turkey Breast with Apple-Onion Stuffing. Treat your brood to an elegant evening with an entree of Chicken Cordon Bleu, Turkey Scaloppine with Parmesan Cheese, or Cranberry Cornish Hens. Or surprise your family with the deliciously different Chicken Wellington, curry-rich Country Captain, or succulent Turkey Forester. From robust family feeds to the exquisite flavors of a more sophisticated sort, these poultry recipes rule the roost.

SAVORY GRILLED CHICKEN WITH MUSTARD SAUCE

SAVORY GRILLED CHICKEN WITH MUSTARD SAUCE

Makes 4 Servings

Basil Butter:

- ¼ cup butter *or* margarine
- 1 teaspoon garlic powder
- 1 teaspoon snipped fresh basil *or* ¼ teaspoon dried basil, crushed
- ¾ teaspoon onion powder

Mustard Sauce:

- ⅓ cup mayonnaise
- 2 tablespoons Dijon-style mustard
- 1½ teaspoons Worcestershire sauce
- ¾ teaspoon dry mustard
- Dash onion powder
- Dash garlic powder
- Dash ground white pepper
- 2 drops bottled hot pepper sauce
- 2 whole large chicken breasts (2 pounds total), skinned, boned and halved lengthwise

◆　　◆　　◆

As well as including many "ravishing" recipes, this cookbook also features a "Food for Fitness" section from the hospital staff physicians.

Stephen Leipre, Executive Chef

Lobster Shanty

Auxili-Ann and Andy's

Ravishing Recipes

Martin Memorial

Hospital Auxiliary

Stuart

FLORIDA

1 To make the Basil Butter: In small saucepan, melt the butter or margarine over low heat. Stir in the 1 teaspoon garlic powder, the basil and the ¾ teaspoon onion powder. Set aside.

2 To make the Mustard Sauce: In a small bowl, stir together the mayonnaise, Dijon-style mustard, Worcestershire sauce, dry mustard, dash onion powder, dash garlic powder, white pepper and hot pepper sauce. Refrigerate the sauce until serving. Or, if you prefer to serve the sauce hot, transfer the mixture to a small saucepan and cook and stir until heated through. Keep warm until serving.

3 Trim any fat from the chicken, rinse and pat dry. Place each breast half, boned side up, between 2 pieces of clear plastic wrap. Working from the center out to the edges, pound lightly with the flat side of a meat mallet to ¼-inch thickness. Remove the plastic wrap.

4 Grill the chicken directly over medium-hot coals for 10 to 12 minutes or until the chicken is tender and no longer pink. Halfway through grilling, turn over the breasts and generously brush each with the Basil Butter. Serve with the Mustard Sauce.

 TIPS FROM OUR KITCHEN

Instead of chopping fresh herbs with a knife, place the leaves in a deep container and snip with a scissors. Snip only the leaves, not the stems.

To avoid flare-ups, only brush the chicken with the Basil Butter once after turning.

Nutrition Analysis: (*Per Serving*): Calories: 370 / Cholesterol: 101 mg / Carbohydrates: 2 g / Protein: 23 g / Sodium: 482 mg / Fat: 30 g (Saturated Fat: 10 g) / Potassium: 225 mg.

CHICKEN PICCATA

Makes 8 Servings

8	medium, boneless, skinless chicken breast halves (1½ pounds)
2	tablespoons lemon juice
2	tablespoons water
½	cup all-purpose flour
¼	teaspoon salt
¼	teaspoon pepper
2	tablespoons olive oil *or* cooking oil
1	tablespoon butter *or* margarine
¾	cup water
⅓	cup dry white wine
1	chicken-flavored bouillon cube *or* 1 teaspoon instant chicken bouillon granules
4	teaspoons all-purpose flour
1	lemon
	Parsley
1	pound fettuccine, cooked and drained and kept warm

◆   ◆   ◆

The Junior Service League of Gainesville, Georgia, is involved in many community service programs. Perennials chairperson, Pat Hensley, reports that the cookbook project has generated over $200,000 toward their efforts.

Dee Lawson Morris
Perennials: A Southern Celebration of Foods and Flavors
The Junior Service League of Gainesville, Georgia
Gainesville
GEORGIA

1 Rinse the chicken and pat dry with paper towels.

2 Place the chicken breast halves, 1 piece at a time, between layers of heavy plastic wrap. Using the flat side of a meat mallet, pound to about ⅛-inch thickness. Remove the plastic wrap and place the chicken in a heavy plastic bag set in a deep bowl.

3 In a small bowl, combine the 2 tablespoons lemon juice and the 2 tablespoons water; pour over the chicken in the bag. Close the bag and marinate at room temperature for 30 minutes. Remove the chicken pieces and discard the marinade.

4 In a shallow dish, stir together the ½ cup flour, the salt and pepper. Dip the chicken in the flour mixture to coat.

5 In a 12-inch skillet, heat the oil and butter or margarine over medium heat. Cook the chicken, *half* at a time, for 6 to 8 minutes or until lightly browned and no pink remains, turning once. Transfer the chicken to a warm serving platter. Cover to keep warm.

6 In a small bowl, stir together the ¾ cup water, the white wine, bouillon cube or granules and the 4 teaspoons flour. Stir the mixture into the drippings in the skillet, scraping to loosen any browned bits. Cook and stir until the mixture is thickened and bubbly. Cook and stir for 1 minute more.

7 Squeeze the juice of *half* of the lemon (about 4 teaspoons) into the sauce in the skillet. Heat through. Pour sauce over the chicken.

8 Thinly slice the remaining lemon half and garnish the serving platter with the lemon slices and parsley. Serve with the hot cooked fettuccine.

 TIPS FROM OUR KITCHEN

If you want to debone and skin the chicken breasts yourself, buy 3 pounds of chicken breasts.

Because chicken is already tender, flatten it with the flat side of a meat mallet, not the ridged side which is designed for tenderizing.

If desired, serve the chicken with spinach noodles or vermicelli instead of fettuccine.

Nutrition Analysis (*Per Serving*): Calories: 398 / Cholesterol: 48 mg / Carbohydrates: 53 g / Protein: 25 g / Sodium: 299 mg / Fat: 8 g (Saturated Fat: 2 g) / Potassium: 208 mg.

CHICKEN PICCATA

HONEY LIME CHICKEN

HONEY LIME CHICKEN

2 tablespoons peanut oil *or* vegetable oil
1 2½- to 3-pound broiler-fryer chicken, cut up
1 tablespoon minced onion
1 clove garlic, minced
2 tablespoons soy sauce
2 tablespoons lime juice
1 tablespoon honey
¼ to ½ teaspoon crushed red pepper flakes
½ teaspoon ground cumin
½ teaspoon ground coriander
¼ teaspoon ground turmeric (optional)
1 lime, thinly sliced

❖ ❖ ❖

The exotic flavors of Indonesian cooking have been "Americanized" in this recipe by Kathy Van Arsdale. While living in Sumatra for 3½ months, her family developed a real taste for the local dishes. Back home in Boulder, Colorado, many ingredients were unavailable, so Kathy improvised.

Kathy Van Arsdale
The Colorado Cook Book
University of Colorado Women's Club—Friends of the Library
Boulder
COLORADO

1 In a heavy 12-inch skillet, heat the oil. Add the chicken pieces with the meaty parts toward the center of the pan where the heat is most intense. Lightly brown the chicken over medium heat for 10 minutes. Push the chicken to one side; add the onion and garlic, and cook and stir for 1 to 2 minutes or until the onion is tender. Drain off the fat and discard.

2 Combine the soy sauce, lime juice, honey, red pepper, cumin, coriander and, if desired, turmeric. Pour the mixture over the chicken, stirring to coat. Cover the skillet and simmer about 35 minutes or until the chicken is tender, turning once. The chicken is done when it feels tender and is easily pierced with a fork. Be sure to test the thigh or breast at a point near the bone, because these parts require the most cooking time.

3 Transfer the chicken to a warm serving dish. Garnish with lime twists. To make lime twists, cut into the center of each lime slice and then twist the ends in opposite directions.

4 Stir the pan juices and spoon over chicken.

TIPS FROM OUR KITCHEN

Remove the skin from the chicken before you start cooking to eliminate some of the fat from this dish.

Don't worry if the meat nearest the bone darkens or is still pink after cooking. This coloring is caused by natural reactions that occur as the chicken cooks. It does not affect the safety or flavor of the chicken.

Nutrient Analysis *(Per Serving)*: Calories: 236 / Cholesterol: 118 mg / Carbohydrates: 9 g / Protein: 38 g / Sodium: 628 mg / Fat: 25 g (Saturated Fat: 6 g) / Potassium: 371 mg.

BAKED CHICKEN WITH CIDER AND APPLES

Makes 6 Servings
- 3 pounds meaty chicken pieces
- 2 cups apple cider
- ½ cup all-purpose flour
- 1 teaspoon ground ginger
- 1 teaspoon ground cinnamon
- ½ teaspoon salt
- ⅛ teaspoon freshly ground pepper
- 1 to 3 tablespoons brown sugar
- 2 tablespoons applejack *or* apple cider
- 2 medium cooking apples, cored and cut into thin wedges

◆　◆　◆

The United Methodist Women's Gourmet Fellowship is a group of people from Nichols United Methodist Church who regularly get together in small groups for dinners. We agree with their philosophy, "There's no better way to get to know someone than to sit across a table from him or her."

United Methodist Women's Gourmet Fellowship
<u>*50th Anniversary Cookbook*</u>
Nichols United Methodist Women
Trumbull
CONNECTICUT

1 Wash the chicken pieces, pat dry and remove the skin and visible fat, if desired. Place the chicken pieces in a large nonmetal bowl or container and pour the cider over the chicken. Cover and refrigerate overnight, turning the pieces occasionally.

2 Preheat the oven to 350°. Remove the chicken from the cider, reserving the cider.

3 In a shallow bowl or plastic bag, combine the flour, ginger, cinnamon, salt and pepper. Coat the chicken pieces with the flour mixture. (If using a plastic bag, add the chicken pieces to the bag, a few at a time. Close the bag and shake to coat the pieces well.)

4 Place the chicken pieces in a single layer in a 3-quart rectangular baking dish. Bake in the 350° oven for 30 minutes.

5 Meanwhile, in a medium mixing bowl, combine *1½ cups* of the reserved cider, the brown sugar and applejack or apple cider. Stir in the apple slices.

6 After the chicken has baked for 30 minutes, pour the apple mixture over it, then continue to bake about 25 minutes more or until the chicken is tender and no longer pink, basting occasionally with the pan juices.

 TIPS FROM OUR KITCHEN

Many varieties of "cooking" apples are available throughout the year and each has a unique flavor. The following tend to be slightly to moderately tart: Baldwin, Cortland, Gravenstein, Grimes Golden, Jonathan, McIntosh, Rome Beauty and Wealthy. If you prefer a sweeter cooking apple, try Golden Delicious, whereas if you prefer a tarter cooking apple, try Winesap.

Nutrition Analysis (*Per Serving*): Calories: 362 / Cholesterol: 104 mg / Carbohydrates: 24 g / Protein: 34 g / Sodium: 273 mg / Fat: 13 g (Saturated Fat: 3 g) Potassium: 424 mg.

BAKED CHICKEN WITH CIDER AND APPLES

COUNTRY-BAKED CHICKEN

COUNTRY-BAKED CHICKEN

Makes 6 Servings
- ¼ cup butter *or* margarine, melted
- ¼ cup all-purpose flour
- ⅛ teaspoon salt
- ⅛ teaspoon pepper
- 3 pounds meaty chicken pieces
- 1 16-ounce jar small whole onions, drained
- 1 4½-ounce jar sliced mushrooms, drained
- 1 12-ounce can evaporated milk
- 1 10¾-ounce can cream of mushroom soup
- 1 cup shredded cheddar cheese (4 ounces)
- 1 teaspoon soy sauce
- ¼ teaspoon pepper

Paprika

◆   ◆   ◆

The Junior League of Rockford has approximately 238 sustainer members. The league's primary focus is on family concerns—specifically health, education and welfare—and their work in these areas has earned them several community service awards.

<u>*Brunch Basket*</u>
The Junior League of Rockford
Rockford
ILLINOIS

1 Preheat the oven to 375°.

2 Pour the melted butter or margarine into a 13x9x2-inch baking pan; set aside.

3 In a small bowl or heavy plastic bag, mix together the flour, salt and the ⅛ teaspoon pepper. Coat the chicken pieces with the seasoned flour mixture and place them in a single layer in the prepared baking pan, skin side down. Bake, uncovered, in the 375° oven for 35 minutes.

4 Remove the pan from the oven. Turn the chicken pieces; pour off and discard the excess fat. Add the onions and mushrooms.

5 In a medium bowl, stir together the evaporated milk, undiluted cream of

mushroom soup, cheddar cheese, soy sauce and the ¼ teaspoon pepper. Pour the milk mixture evenly over the chicken, onions and mushrooms. Sprinkle with the paprika. Cover the dish loosely with aluminum foil and continue baking for 15 to 20 minutes more or until the sauce is heated through and the chicken pieces are tender and no longer pink.

 TIPS FROM OUR KITCHEN

To coat the chicken pieces with a minimum amount of fuss and muss, place the seasoned flour in a heavy plastic bag. Add a few of the chicken pieces at a time, seal the bag and carefully shake until evenly coated.

If desired, substitute boiling onions for the jarred onions. Before adding them to the chicken, cook 1 pound of boiling onions in water until they are tender. Then, remove the outer skins.

If you wish, you can reduce the fat and sodium in this recipe. To reduce the fat: Remove the skin from the chicken pieces before baking, eliminate the ¼ cup butter or margarine, bake the chicken in a covered pan that has been sprayed with nonstick vegetable coating and use evaporated skim milk and/or low-fat cheese. To lower the sodium, use low-sodium soup, cheddar cheese and soy sauce.

Nutrition Analysis (*Per Serving*): Calories: 556 / Cholesterol: 161 mg / Carbohydrates: 15 g / Protein: 44 g / Sodium: 991 mg / Fat: 35 g (Saturated Fat: 16 g) / Potassium: 549 mg.

BUTTERMILK FRIED CHICKEN AND BISCUITS

Makes 6 Servings

Chicken:
- 1 3- to 3½-pound broiler-fryer chicken, cut up
- ¾ cup buttermilk
- ½ cup all-purpose flour
- 2 tablespoons snipped parsley
- 1 teaspoon dried oregano, crushed
- ½ teaspoon salt
- ½ teaspoon pepper
- ¼ cup shortening
- ¼ cup margarine *or* butter
- Melted margarine *or* butter
- ¼ cup chicken broth

Biscuits:
- 2 cups all-purpose flour
- 1 tablespoon sugar
- 2½ teaspoons baking powder
- ½ teaspoon baking soda
- ½ teaspoon salt
- ¾ cup buttermilk

♦ ♦ ♦

The Church of the Redeemer collected recipes from parish members and residents of the Camelot Nursing Home in Richmond, Virginia, for ...And These Thy Gifts. All profits from cookbook sales were donated to the Camelot Nursing Home to help purchase recreation equipment.

Cookie Suarez
...And These Thy Gifts
Church of the Redeemer
Mechanicsville
VIRGINIA

1 Rinse the chicken pieces; pat dry. Place the chicken pieces in a 3-quart rectangular baking dish. Pour the ¾ cup buttermilk over the chicken; cover and let stand for 30 minutes to 1 hour in the refrigerator.

2 About 10 minutes before removing the chicken from the refrigerator: In a shallow dish, stir together the ½ cup flour, the parsley, oregano, the ½ teaspoon salt and the pepper.

3 Remove the chicken from the baking dish, reserving the buttermilk. Coat the chicken with the flour mixture.

4 In a 12-inch skillet over medium heat, melt the shortening and the ¼ cup margarine or butter. Brown the chicken pieces in the skillet for 10 minutes, turning once. Drain and transfer the chicken to the baking dish, placing the pieces in the reserved buttermilk.

5 Strain the drippings from the skillet into a measuring cup. If necessary, add additional melted margarine or butter to make ⅓ cup. Reserve for the biscuits.

6 Preheat the oven to 375°.

7 Add the chicken broth to the skillet, scraping the bottom of the pan to loosen any browned bits. Pour the mixture evenly over the chicken in the baking dish. Bake, uncovered, in the 375° oven about 50 minutes or until the chicken is tender and no longer pink.

8 Meanwhile, to make the biscuits: In a medium bowl, stir together the 2 cups flour, the sugar, baking powder, baking soda and the ½ teaspoon salt. Add the reserved drippings and the ¾ cup buttermilk. Stir just until the dough clings together.

9 On a lightly floured surface, knead the dough gently for 10 to 12 strokes. Roll or pat the dough to ½-inch thickness. Using a 2-inch biscuit cutter, cut the dough into rounds. Transfer the biscuits to a baking sheet. Bake in the 375° oven for 15 to 20 minutes or until golden. Serve warm with the Buttermilk Fried Chicken.

 TIPS FROM OUR KITCHEN

To cut up a whole chicken: First remove the thighs and the legs by bending at the hip joints. Pull the wings away from the body and slit the skin between the wing and the body. Bend the wing back until the joint breaks. Using a sharp knife or kitchen shears, cut along the breast end of the ribs; bend the 2 halves apart and cut through the neck joints. Bend the 2 halves of the chicken back toward the skin side until the bones break. Cut in half and cut off the tail. Cut the breast in half lengthwise along the breastbone.

Nutrition Analysis (*Per Serving*): Calories: 573 / Cholesterol: 81 mg / Carbohydrates: 43 g / Protein: 32 g / Sodium: 725 mg / Fat: 30 g (Saturated Fat: 7 g) / Potassium: 414 mg.

BUTTERMILK FRIED CHICKEN AND BISCUITS

OVEN SESAME CHICKEN

OVEN SESAME CHICKEN

Makes 6 Servings
- 1   2½- to 3-pound broiler-fryer chicken, cut up
- ⅓   cup all-purpose flour
- 2½   teaspoons paprika
- 1   teaspoon seasoned salt
- ¼   teaspoon pepper
- 3   eggs
- 4   teaspoons water
- 3   tablespoons toasted sesame seed

◆   ◆   ◆

Since the eruption of Mt. St. Helens in 1981, the influx of visitors to the area has placed an added burden on the all-volunteer Cowlitz County Fire District #7. To raise much-needed funds, Volcanic Concoctions was created. About her own particular concoction, Ilene Black says that it is fast becoming a family favorite. She has passed the recipe along to her daughters, and her grandchildren are always asking, "When is Grandma going to make Sesame Chicken?"

Ilene Black
Volcanic Concoctions
Cowlitz County Fire District #7
Ariel
WASHINGTON

1 Rinse the chicken and pat dry. Preheat the oven to 350°. Grease a 3-quart rectangular baking dish. Set aside.

2 On a piece of waxed paper, combine the flour, paprika, seasoned salt and pepper. In a medium mixing bowl, beat together the eggs and water.

3 Dip the chicken pieces, one at a time, in the egg mixture, then in the seasoned flour. Dip the chicken again in the egg mixture, then sprinkle with the sesame seed.

4 Arrange the coated chicken pieces in a single layer in the prepared baking dish. Bake in the 350° oven for 50 to 60 minutes or until the chicken is brown, crisp and tender. To check for doneness, cut into a thick piece up to the bone. If no pink remains, the chicken is done. Serve the chicken hot or cold.

 TIPS FROM OUR KITCHEN

To toast the sesame seed: Spread it in a thin layer in a shallow, ungreased baking pan and bake in a 350° oven for 10 to 15 minutes or until golden, stirring once or twice.

To cut up a chicken: First remove the legs by cutting through the skin between the thigh and the body. Bend the thigh back until the hip joint breaks, then cut through the joint. Bend the knee joint to break it, then cut apart the thigh and drumstick.

Next, remove the wings by pulling each away from the body. Slit the skin between the wing and the body, bending to break the joint and then cutting through it.

To separate the breast from the back, use a sharp knife or kitchen shears to cut toward the neck along the breast end of the ribs on one side. Bend the halves apart, then cut through the neck joints.

To halve the breast, cut it lengthwise along the breastbone. If desired, remove the skin from each piece.

After cutting up chicken or other raw meat, scrub the cutting board with hot, soapy water before using it for vegetables or other foods.

Nutrition Analysis (*Per Serving*): Calories: 265 / Cholesterol: 172 mg / Carbohydrates: 6 g / Protein: 25 g / Sodium: 311 mg / Fat: 15 g (Saturated Fat: 4 g) / Potassium: 242 mg.

CRUNCHY CHICKEN

Makes 6 Servings

- 6   skinless, boneless chicken breast halves
- 1   8-ounce carton dairy sour cream
- 2   tablespoons lemon juice
- 2   teaspoons Worcestershire sauce
- 1   teaspoon celery seed
- 1   teaspoon paprika
- ½   teaspoon garlic powder
- ⅛   teaspoon pepper
- 2   cups herb stuffing mix, crushed
- ¼   cup margarine *or* butter, melted

◆   ◆   ◆

The Philadelphia Rotary Club established a fund-raising goal of $120 million to be used toward the fight against polio. Their cookbook, What's Cooking in Philadelphia*, far exceeded those expectations. It includes typical Philadelphian dishes, as well as many recipes that represent the "wonderful diversity of ethnic backgrounds reflecting the City of Philadelphia."*

Mary Plakis
What's Cooking in Philadelphia
The Philadelphia Rotary Club
Philadelphia
PENNSYLVANIA

1 Preheat the oven to 375°. Rinse the chicken and pat dry with paper towels.

2 In a medium bowl, stir together the sour cream, lemon juice, Worcestershire sauce, celery seed, paprika, garlic powder and pepper.

3 Place the crushed herb stuffing mix in a shallow pie plate. Dip the chicken in the sour cream mixture, coating both sides of each piece. Roll the coated chicken in the crushed herb stuffing mix.

4 Place the coated chicken in a 15x10x1-inch baking pan. Drizzle the melted margarine or butter over the chicken.

5 Bake the chicken in the 375° oven for 20 to 25 minutes or until the chicken is no longer pink in the center.

 TIPS FROM OUR KITCHEN

For the crispiest coating, bake the chicken breasts immediately after rolling them in the crushed stuffing.

For a change of taste, try using crushed corn bread stuffing instead of the herb stuffing mix in this recipe.

Turkey tenderloins can be used instead of the chicken breasts in this recipe.

Nutrition Analysis (*Per Serving*): Calories: 231 / Cholesterol: 59 mg / Carbohydrates: 8 g / Protein: 23 g / Sodium: 297 mg / Fat: 11 g (Saturated Fat: 2 g) / Potassium: 222 mg.

CRUNCHY CHICKEN

CHICKEN WELLINGTON

CHICKEN WELLINGTON

Makes 8 Servings

- 4 whole medium chicken breasts, skinned and halved lengthwise
- 6 tablespoons lemon juice
- 2 tablespoons butter *or* margarine
- 1 large onion, finely chopped (¾ cup)
- 1 large shallot, finely chopped
- 1 10¾-ounce can condensed cream of mushroom soup
- 2 tablespoons snipped fresh cilantro
- ¼ teaspoon pepper
- 1 17½-ounce package (2 sheets) frozen puff pastry, thawed
- 2 egg yolks, beaten
- 2 tablespoons butter *or* margarine
- 1 large shallot, finely chopped
- 1 cup sliced fresh mushrooms
- ½ cup dry white wine

About twenty years ago, when the

◆　◆　◆

town of Rancho Santa Fe was very rural and there were no markets nearby, resident Rochelle Green wanted to make Beef Wellington. When she realized she had no beef, she substituted chicken and created this great recipe for Chicken Wellington.

Rochelle Green
The Country Friends
The Country Friends, Inc.
Rancho Santa Fe
CALIFORNIA

1 Preheat the oven to 350°. Rinse the chicken breasts. Place the chicken in a 3-quart rectangular baking dish. Sprinkle with the lemon juice. Cover and bake in the 350° oven for 45 to 60 minutes or until the chicken is tender and no longer pink. Cool slightly. Remove the bones, keeping the meat in large pieces. Increase the oven temperature to 450°.

2 In a large skillet, heat the 2 tablespoons butter or margarine. Add the onion and shallot and cook until tender. Stir in the undiluted mushroom soup, the cilantro and pepper. Simmer, uncovered, for 5 to 10 minutes. Remove from heat; cool.

3 Meanwhile, on a lightly floured surface, roll *each* sheet of thawed pastry to a 12-inch square. Cut each pastry sheet into four 6-inch squares. Place 1 cooked chicken breast half in the center of each square. Spoon about *2 tablespoons* of the soup mixture onto each piece of chicken.

4 Brush the edges of the pastry with *water*. Wrap the pastry around the chicken, pressing the edges neatly and firmly together.

5 Place the pastry-wrapped chicken pieces, seam side down, on a lightly greased baking sheet. Brush with beaten egg yolk. Bake, uncovered, in the 450° oven for 10 minutes. Reduce heat to 425°; bake about 10 minutes more or until pastry is golden brown.

6 Meanwhile, in a medium skillet, heat the 2 tablespoons butter or margarine. Add the finely chopped shallot and cook for 2 minutes. Add the sliced mushrooms and cook for 2 minutes. Add the wine and simmer, uncovered, for 5 minutes. Top each serving with the mushroom sauce.

 TIPS FROM OUR KITCHEN

If desired, the pastry-wrapped chicken can be placed in freezer containers and frozen. Place frozen pastry-wrapped chicken pieces on a greased baking sheet. Brush with the beaten egg yolks. Bake in a 375° oven for 25 to 30 minutes or until pastry is golden brown.

Nutrition Analysis (*Per Serving*): Calories: 487 / Cholesterol: 114 mg / Carbohydrates: 28 g / Protein: 21 g / Sodium: 642 mg / Fat: 31 g (Saturated Fat: 5 g) / Potassium: 258 mg.

CHICKEN BREASTS STUFFED WITH SPINACH AND MUSHROOMS

Makes 4 Servings

- 2 whole medium chicken breasts (1½ pounds total), skinned, boned and halved lengthwise
- 10 ounces fresh spinach
- 2 cups thinly sliced fresh mushrooms
- ¼ cup finely chopped onion
- ¼ teaspoon minced garlic
- ⅛ teaspoon ground nutmeg
- 1 tablespoon butter *or* margarine

Salt

Pepper

- 1 cup tomato sauce

Grated Parmesan cheese

Fresh basil *or* parsley sprigs

◆　　◆　　◆

Clare Furnary told us that this is an excellent recipe because it always "turns out perfect and can be served as a gourmet, company or family dish." She also said that when the leftovers are "sliced and put on a bed of lettuce for a luncheon salad" they are just as tasty as the original dish.

Clare Furnary
Birthright Sampler: A Melting Pot of Ethnic Recipes
Birthright of Johnstown, Inc.
Johnstown
PENNSYLVANIA

1 Preheat the oven to 425°.

2 Rinse the chicken breast halves; pat dry. Place the breast halves, boned side up, between 2 pieces of heavy-duty, clear plastic wrap. Working from the center out to the edges, lightly pound the chicken with the flat side of a meat mallet to form ⅛-inch-thick rectangles. Remove the plastic wrap.

3 Cook the spinach in enough *boiling water* to cover until wilted; drain well. Coarsely chop the spinach; set aside.

4 In a large skillet, cook *half* of the mushrooms, *half* of the onion, the garlic and nutmeg in the butter or margarine until the vegetables are tender. Stir in the spinach.

 TIPS FROM OUR KITCHEN

To save last minute preparation time, rinse and flatten the chicken breast halves earlier in the day or the night before. Wrap each chicken breast half in the plastic wrap, place the wrapped chicken breasts in a plastic bag or

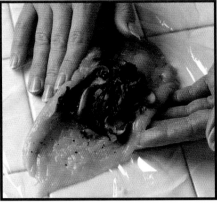

5 Sprinkle the chicken breast halves with salt and pepper. Spoon equal portions of the spinach-mushroom mixture into the center of *each* chicken breast. Fold in the long sides of each chicken breast and roll up jelly-roll fashion. Secure each chicken roll with a wooden toothpick.

6 Place the chicken rolls, seam side down, in a shallow baking dish. Sprinkle the remaining mushrooms and onion around the chicken rolls.

7 Bake the chicken rolls in the 425° oven for 10 minutes. Spoon the tomato sauce around the chicken rolls and bake, basting occasionally, for 10 to 15 minutes more or until the chicken is tender and no pink remains. Sprinkle the chicken rolls with the Parmesan cheese. Garnish with the basil or parsley sprigs.

covered container and refrigerate. You can also prepare the spinach and chop the onion ahead of time.

Serve the chicken rolls with spinach fettuccine or your favorite cooked rice.

Nutrition Analysis (*Per Serving*): Calories: 174 / Cholesterol: 55 mg / Carbohydrates: 9 g / Protein: 21 g / Sodium: 555 mg / Fat: 7 g (Saturated Fat: 3 g) / Potassium: 748 mg.

Chicken Breasts Stuffed with Spinach and Mushrooms

CHICKEN CORDON BLEU

CHICKEN CORDON BLEU

Makes 6 Servings

3	medium whole chicken breasts, skinned, boned and halved lengthwise
6	slices fully cooked ham (about 6 ounces)
12	thin slices Swiss cheese (about 6 ounces)
2	eggs, beaten
2	tablespoons dry white wine
½	cup all-purpose flour
1	cup fine dry bread crumbs
¼	cup margarine *or* butter
8	ounces fresh shiitake *and/or* button mushrooms, sliced (3 cups)
2	10¾-ounce cans condensed cream of mushroom soup
1¼	cups milk (1 soup can full)
¼	cup dry white wine

♦ ♦ ♦

Janet Alcott told us that this elegant, yet easy recipe was one of her husband's favorite dishes; he loved the ham, cheese and chicken combination. A teacher of 34 years, Janet enjoys entertaining her school colleagues and friends, and she finds that this is still the dish she prepares most often for her dinner parties.

Janet Alcott
<u>Mark Twain Library Cookbook</u>
The Mark Twain Library
Association
Redding
CONNECTICUT

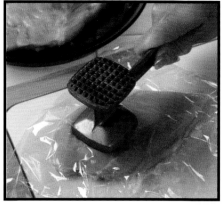

1 Rinse the chicken breasts; pat dry. Place each breast half, boned side up, between 2 pieces of clear heavy-duty plastic wrap. Working from the center to the edges, lightly pound with the flat side of a meat mallet to a ⅛-inch thickness. Remove the plastic wrap.

2 Place *1* slice of ham and *2* slices of Swiss cheese on *each* piece of chicken, folding the ham and cheese if necessary to fit on the chicken.

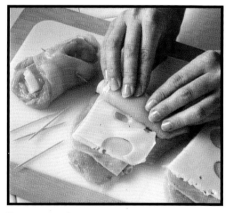

3 Starting from one short side, roll up each piece of chicken, jelly-roll fashion, and secure with wooden toothpicks.

4 In a shallow dish, stir together the beaten eggs and the 2 tablespoons white wine. Roll *each* chicken bundle in the flour, dip in the egg mixture and coat with the bread crumbs. Preheat the oven to 325°.

5 In a large skillet, melt the margarine or butter. Lightly brown the chicken on all sides. Remove the chicken from the skillet; reserve the drippings.

6 Transfer the chicken to a 3-quart rectangular baking dish and carefully remove the toothpicks.

7 Cook the mushrooms in the skillet with the reserved drippings for 4 to 5 minutes or until tender. Add the undiluted cream of mushroom soup and milk to the skillet. Stir until well mixed.

8 Remove the soup-milk mixture from the heat and stir in the ¼ cup white wine. Pour the sauce over the chicken in the baking dish. Bake in the 325° oven about 45 minutes or until the chicken is tender and no longer pink.

 TIPS FROM OUR KITCHEN

Serve this saucy chicken dish with cooked spinach or egg noodles or with a mixture of wild and brown rice.

Remember the "hot foods hot" rule if you plan to serve this dish at a buffet. Make sure your warming tray is working properly and plan the baking time so that the chicken is done as close to serving time as possible.

Nutrition Analysis (*Per Serving*): Calories: 578 / Cholesterol: 155 mg / Carbohydrates: 33 g / Protein: 40 g / Sodium: 1518 mg / Fat: 31 g (Saturated Fat: 11 g) / Potassium: 607 mg.

COUNTRY CAPTAIN

Makes 4 to 6 Servings

1	2½- to 3-pound broiler-fryer chicken, cut up
½	teaspoon salt
¼	teaspoon white or black pepper
2	tablespoons cooking oil
2	cups finely chopped onion
2	cups finely chopped green sweet pepper
1	large garlic clove, minced
1 to 2	teaspoons curry powder
1	16-ounce can tomatoes, cut up
2	tablespoons snipped parsley
¼	teaspoon dried thyme, crushed
⅛	teaspoon white *or* black pepper
3	tablespoons currants
¼	cup toasted slivered almonds

❖   ❖   ❖

Mrs. Willaim Bullard of Warm Springs, Georgia, needed a special dish to serve at a dinner for her famous neighbor, Franklin Delano Roosevelt, so she created this variation of a classic chicken dish. Now we share this dish with you courtesy of Mrs. Bullard's daughter, Mrs. Leighton W. McPherson.

Mrs. Leighton W. McPherson
A Southern Collection
Columbus
GEORGIA

1 Preheat oven to 350°.

2 Sprinkle the chicken with the salt and the ¼ teaspoon pepper. In a heavy 12-inch skillet, cook the chicken in the oil about 5 minutes per side or until it is browned. Transfer the chicken to a 13x9x2-inch baking pan.

3 Pour off most of the oil from the skillet. Cook and stir the onion, sweet pepper and garlic over low heat, until the onion is translucent. Stir in the curry powder. Add the tomatoes, *1 tablespoon* of the parsley, the thyme and the ⅛ teaspoon pepper to the skillet. Bring the mixture to a boil. Pour the sauce over the chicken in the pan.

4 Cover and bake the chicken in the 350° oven for 45 minutes; uncover and bake for 15 minutes more.

5 Place the chicken on a large warm platter. Skim any fat from the sauce. Stir the currants into the sauce and pour some over the chicken. Sprinkle the almonds and remaining parsley over the chicken. Serve the remaining sauce on the side.

To cut up canned tomatoes quickly and easily, we use sharp kitchen scissors and cut them right in the can.

In India, the spices that go into curry depend on the cook and can be a blend of as many as 16 different spices. If you'd like to make your own, try the following combination:

2	tablespoons ground coriander
5	teaspoons ground turmeric
1	tablespoon ground cardamom
1	tablespoon ground cumin
1	tablespoon ground fenugreek
1	teaspoon black pepper
1	teaspoon ground red pepper
½	teaspoon ground cinnamon
½	teaspoon ground cloves
½	teaspoon crushed fennel
½	teaspoon ground ginger.

We suggest you serve Country Captain over fluffy rice and garnish with fresh parsley.

Nutrition Analysis (*Per Serving,*): Calories: 437 / Cholesterol: 99 mg / Carbohydrates: 17 g / Protein: 34 g / Sodium: 547 mg / Fat: 26 g (Saturated Fat: 6 g) / Potassium: 739 mg.

COUNTRY CAPTAIN

CHICKEN WITH JULIENNE PEPPERS

CHICKEN WITH JULIENNE PEPPERS

Makes 6 Servings

6	chicken breast halves (about 3 pounds total)
2	tablespoons olive oil
1	cup finely chopped onion
2	carrots, finely chopped
4	cloves garlic, minced
1	14½-ounce can whole Italian-style tomatoes, cut up
1	cup chicken broth
½	cup orange juice
1	teaspoon dried rosemary, crushed
1	red sweet pepper, cut into julienne strips
1	green sweet pepper, cut into julienne strips
1	yellow sweet pepper, cut into julienne strips
2	tablespoons snipped parsley

◆   ◆   ◆

Now in its second printing, <u>Gateways</u> has sold 15,000 copies. Suzanne Boyle, cookbook chairperson, told us that after they have sold the remaining 4,900 cookbooks, the organization might reprint, "if the demand is still there and they continue to sell as fast as they are now."

<u>Gateways</u>
Auxiliary Twigs…Friends of the
St. Louis Children's Hospital
St. Louis
MISSOURI

1 If desired, skin the chicken breast halves. Rinse the chicken under cold running water; pat dry. Sprinkle the chicken with ¼ teaspoon *salt* and ⅛ teaspoon *freshly ground pepper*.

2 In a 12-inch skillet over medium heat, heat the olive oil until hot. Add the chicken to the skillet; cook about 10 minutes or until golden, turning occasionally. Transfer the chicken to a plate; reserve the drippings.

3 Add the onion, carrots and garlic to the reserved drippings; reduce heat to low. Cover and cook about 5 minutes or until the vegetables are crisp-tender.

4 Carefully add the *undrained* tomatoes, chicken broth, orange juice and rosemary. Add the browned chicken breasts to the skillet and simmer for 30 minutes.

5 Add the julienned red, green and yellow sweet peppers to the chicken mixture. Cover and simmer for 5 to 10 minutes more or until the sweet peppers are crisp-tender and the chicken is no longer pink.

6 Remove the chicken from the skillet. Ladle the vegetable mixture into serving bowls; top each serving with a chicken breast half. Sprinkle with parsley.

 TIPS FROM OUR KITCHEN

You'll need 1 large or 2 medium onions to yield the 1 cup of chopped onion called for in this recipe.

If fresh rosemary is available, substitute 1 tablespoon of fresh rosemary for the 1 teaspoon of dried rosemary.

Julienne strips can be as thin as matchsticks. Cut each pepper in half and then cut into ⅛- to ¼-inch-thick slices.

Try serving this dish with garlic toast. Combine 2 tablespoons *olive oil* and 2 cloves minced *garlic*. Brush the garlic mixture on six 1-inch-thick slices of French bread. Broil the slices 3 to 4 inches from the heat source for 2 to 3 minutes or until the toast is golden.

Other great choices for side dishes are boiled new potatoes, cooked rice, bulgur or pasta.

Nutrition Analysis (*Per Serving*): Calories: 356 / Cholesterol: 104 mg / Carbohydrates: 16 g / Protein: 40 g / Sodium: 435 mg / Fat: 15 g (Saturated Fat: 3 g) / Potassium: 766 mg.

PASTA WITH CHICKEN AND DRIED TOMATOES

Makes 4 Servings

1	pound boneless chicken breasts
2	tablespoons all-purpose flour
2	tablespoons olive oil
3	tablespoons dry white wine
1	cup heavy whipping cream
1	tablespoon Dijon-style mustard
¼	teaspoon salt
⅛	teaspoon pepper
8 to 10	dried tomatoes packed in olive oil, drained and coarsely chopped (⅓ cup)
12	ounces fresh pasta *or* 6 ounces dried pasta, cooked and drained

◆　　◆　　◆

This recipe for Pasta with Chicken and Dried Tomatoes evolved from a dish that Mary James Lawrence used to instruct her cooking class. After an enthusiastic response from her class, she, Linda Lee and Harrison Turner—all owners of Cook's Corner specialty shop—submitted it to Bravo.

Mary James Lawrence
Linda Lee
Harrison Turner, M.D.
Bravo!
Greensboro
NORTH CAROLINA

1 Cut the chicken into bite-size strips. Toss lightly with the flour.

2 In a large skillet, heat the olive oil over medium heat. Add the chicken and cook and stir for 3 to 4 minutes or until the chicken is no longer pink. Remove the chicken from the pan.

3 Add the wine to the pan and deglaze by stirring up any browned bits. Add the whipping cream, mustard, salt and pepper. Bring to a boil. Cook and stir for 3 minutes. Add the tomatoes and continue to cook for 1 to 2 minutes more or until the mixture is slightly thickened.

4 Return the chicken to the pan. Cook until the chicken is just heated through.

5 Pour the chicken and sauce over the hot cooked pasta. Toss and place in large decorative serving bowl.

 TIPS FROM OUR KITCHEN

To save calories and fat, use packaged dried tomatoes rather than those bottled in oil. To soften the dried tomatoes, soak them in boiling water for 2 minutes. Drain well.

To make clean-up a snap, toss the chicken pieces with the flour in a plastic bag.

For a colorful presentation, use half spinach pasta and half regular pasta.

A green salad or a side dish of cooked fresh snow peas or broccoli makes a perfect accompaniment to this dish.

Nutrition Analysis *(Per Serving)*: Calories: 715 / Cholesterol: 214 mg / Carbohydrates: 63 g / Protein: 36 g / Sodium: 410 mg / Fat: 35 g (Saturated Fat: 16 g) / Potassium: 443 mg.

PASTA WITH CHICKEN AND DRIED TOMATOES

CHICKEN WITH ROSEMARY AND GARLIC

CHICKEN WITH ROSEMARY AND GARLIC

Makes 5 to 6 Servings

¼	cup olive oil
1	2½- to 3-pound broiler-fryer chicken *or* roasting hen
Several sprigs fresh rosemary	
1	tablespoon butter *or* margarine
½	teaspoon salt
⅛	teaspoon pepper
2	pounds small new red potatoes
30 to 40	cloves garlic, unpeeled
¼	teaspoon pepper

◆　◆　◆

Thirty-three local cooks and a small group of The Watch Hill Improvement Society family and friends served as the recipe selection committee for Watch Hill Cooks. Each submission was prepared, tested and graded, with only the best recipes included in the cookbook. There is even an "Animal Fare" section—one of the taste testers for this section was Cassie, a committee member's dog!

Watch Hill Cooks
The Watch Hill Improvement Society
Watch Hill
RHODE ISLAND

1 Preheat the oven to 375°.

2 Pour *2 tablespoons* of the olive oil in a 15½x10½x2-inch roasting pan; set aside.

3 Rinse the chicken inside and out; pat dry. Stuff a *few* sprigs of rosemary inside the cavity along with the butter or margarine. Sprinkle with *¼ teaspoon* of the salt and the ⅛ teaspoon pepper. Place the chicken in the prepared roasting pan, breast side up.

4 Scrub the potatoes, leaving them whole. Place the potatoes and the unpeeled garlic around the chicken. Sprinkle the potatoes with the remaining salt and the ¼ teaspoon pepper. Tuck rosemary sprigs all around the chicken among the potatoes and garlic. Drizzle the remaining olive oil over all.

5 Roast the chicken, uncovered, in the 375° oven for 10 minutes. Reduce heat to 350° and roast for 50 to 70 minutes more or until the chicken is no longer pink, turning the chicken and potatoes regularly so they crisp evenly. Transfer the chicken to a serving platter. With a slotted spoon, transfer the potatoes and garlic to the platter. Discard the baked rosemary and garnish with fresh rosemary, if desired.

 TIPS FROM OUR KITCHEN

Squeeze each roasted garlic clove with your fingers to free the garlic from its jacket.

Nutrition Analysis (*Per Serving*): Calories: 502 / Cholesterol: 78mg / Carbohydrates: 50g / Protein: 30g / Sodium: 304mg / Fat: 21g (Saturated Fat: 5g) / Potassium: 1079 mg.

CRANBERRY CORNISH HENS

Makes 4 Servings
- ⅔ cup chopped cranberries
- 2 tablespoons sugar
- 1 teaspoon finely shredded orange peel
- ¼ teaspoon salt
- ⅛ teaspoon ground cinnamon
- 3 cups toasted raisin bread cubes (4 slices)
- ¼ cup butter *or* margarine, melted
- 4 teaspoons orange juice
- 4 Cornish game hens (1¼ to 1½ pounds)
- Cooking oil
- ¼ cup orange juice

◆   ◆   ◆

The East Hawaii Special Olympics Cookbook is dedicated to all cooks. This collection of recipes includes treasured family keepsakes as well as new inventions. All, however, reflect the love of good cooking. The recipe for Cranberry Cornish Hens is one of the cookbook's delicious offerings.

<u>Special Olympics Cookbook</u>
Special Olympics East Hawaii
Hilo
HAWAII

1 Preheat oven to 375°. In a medium bowl, combine the cranberries, sugar, orange peel, salt and cinnamon. Add the bread cubes; drizzle with *half* the melted butter and the 4 teaspoons orange juice. Toss to mix.

2 Rinse the Cornish hens and pat dry. Rub the cavities with the salt.

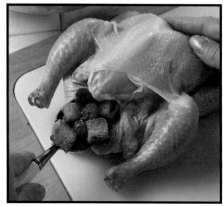

3 Stuff the cavity of each Cornish hen with the cranberry mixture.

4 Skewer the neck skin to the back. Tie the legs to the tail; twist the wings under the back. Place the hens, breast side up, on a rack in a roasting pan. Brush with oil; cover loosely with foil.

5 Roast the Cornish Hens in the 375° oven for 30 minutes.

6 Combine the ¼ cup orange juice and remaining melted butter. Uncover the birds and roast about 45 minutes more or until done, basting once or twice with the orange juice mixture.

 TIPS FROM OUR KITCHEN

To make dry bread cubes for stuffing, cut the bread into ½-inch cubes. (Use 6 slices of bread for 3 cups of dry cubes.) Spread the bread cubes in a single layer in a shallow baking pan. Bake in a 300° oven for 10 to 15 minutes or until dry, stirring twice. Or, let the bread cubes stand, covered, at room temperature for 8 to 12 hours.

If your family members or guests can't handle a whole Cornish hen each, serve half of a bird to each person. To make sure you have enough cranberry stuffing, double the recipe and stuff the birds. Then, add a little more orange juice or water to the remaining stuffing and place it in a covered casserole. Place the extra stuffing in the oven with the birds during the last 20 or 30 minutes of roasting.

For a special presentation, garnish the Cranberry Cornish Hens with cranberry-centered kumquat roses as pictured on the front.

Nutrition Analysis (*Per Serving*): Calories: 931 / Cholesterol: 271 mg / Carbohydrates: 24 g / Protein: 74 g / Sodium: 525 mg / Fat: 61 g (Saturated Fat: 18 g) / Potassium: 114 mg.

CRANBERRY CORNISH HENS

ROAST TURKEY BREAST WITH APPLE-ONION STUFFING

ROAST TURKEY BREAST WITH APPLE-ONION STUFFING

Makes 8 Servings

Apple-Onion Stuffing:
- ¼ cup butter *or* margarine, cut up
- 2 Golden Delicious apples, cored and chopped (2 to 2½ cups)
- 1 cup chopped onion
- ½ cup apple cider
- 2½ cups unseasoned dry bread cubes
- ¼ cup currants *or* raisins
- 2 tablespoons lemon juice
- ½ teaspoon salt
- ¼ teaspoon ground nutmeg
- ¼ teaspoon ground allspice

Turkey:
- 1 5-pound bone-in turkey breast, thawed if necessary
- ½ lemon
- ½ teaspoon salt
- ¼ teaspoon freshly ground pepper
- 2 tablespoons butter *or* margarine, melted

❖   ❖   ❖

Sally Higgins told us that she's such a recipe junkie that she reads recipes in bed at night. "It's the best way to go to sleep. I find it very relaxing."

Sally Higgins
Gateways
Auxiliary Twigs…Friends of the
St. Louis Children's Hospital
St. Louis
MISSOURI

1 To make the Apple-Onion Stuffing: In a large heavy skillet over medium-high heat, melt the ¼ cup butter or margarine. Add the apples, onion and ¼ *cup* of the apple cider. Bring the mixture to a boil. Reduce heat; cover and cook for 5 to 7 minutes or until the apples are tender, stirring occasionally. Transfer the mixture to a large bowl. Stir in the bread cubes.

2 In a small saucepan, stir together the currants or raisins and the remaining apple cider. Bring the mixture to a boil. Reduce heat to low; cover and simmer for 3 to 5 minutes or until the currants are plump. Add the currants and liquid to the stuffing mixture. Add the lemon juice, the ½ teaspoon salt, the nutmeg and allspice. Toss to mix all of the ingredients.

3 Preheat the oven to 325°.

4 To prepare the turkey: Rinse the turkey breast and pat dry with paper towels. Rub the skin and cavity with the lemon half and sprinkle with the ½ teaspoon salt and the pepper. Turn the turkey breast skin side down. Loosely fill the cavity with the Apple-Onion Stuffing. Place any remaining stuffing in a small casserole and bake, covered, during the last 30 minutes of roasting.

5 Place a sheet of aluminum foil firmly over the stuffing in the turkey breast. Turn the turkey breast over to pinch the ends of the aluminum foil together.

6 Place the turkey breast, skin side up, in a shallow roasting pan and brush with the 2 tablespoons melted butter or margarine. Roast the turkey in the 325° oven for 1½ to 2¼ hours or until a thermometer inserted into the thickest part of the breast registers 170° to 175°. Remove the stuffing from the cavity; keep warm. Let the turkey breast stand for 20 minutes at room temperature before carving.

 TIPS FROM OUR KITCHEN

Do not try to save time by stuffing the turkey breast the day before cooking. The meat insulates the stuffing so it doesn't chill as quickly, making the stuffing a prime breeding ground for the bacteria that causes food poisoning.

Nutrition Analysis (*Per Serving*): Calories: 323 / Cholesterol: 87 mg / Carbohydrates: 19 g / Protein: 26 g / Sodium: 489 mg / Fat: 16 g (Saturated Fat: 7 g) / Potassium: 391 mg.

GRILLED TURKEY BREAST

Makes 8 Servings
- ¼ cup cooking oil
- ¼ cup lemon juice
- ¾ teaspoon salt
- ½ teaspoon paprika
- ½ teaspoon dried oregano, crushed
- ¼ teaspoon garlic powder *or* 1 clove garlic, minced
- ¼ teaspoon pepper
- 1 2½-pound boneless turkey breast half
- Fresh thyme sprigs (optional)

◆   ◆   ◆

Marlene Tropper and a friend "from up north" were invited to a barbecue about eight years ago. As their contribution to the meal, the twosome decided to experiment with cooking turkey breasts. They brought their creation, Grilled Turkey Breast, to the barbecue, and everyone— including "some people who don't even like turkey"—loved it. We think you will too!

Marlene Tropper
<u>*Chef's EscOrt*</u>
Women's American Organization for Rehabilitation Through Training
Hollandale
FLORIDA

1 In a small saucepan, stir together the oil, lemon juice, salt, paprika, oregano, garlic powder or minced garlic and pepper. Bring to a boil. Reduce heat and simmer, covered, for 10 minutes. Cool.

2 Rinse the turkey; pat dry with paper towels. Place the turkey in a large plastic bag and set in a deep bowl. Pour the cooled marinade over the turkey in the bag, turning to cover all sides of the turkey. Seal the bag and refrigerate for at least 2 hours, turning occasionally.

3 In a covered grill, arrange coals around a drip pan. Test for medium heat above the drip pan.

4 Drain the turkey and discard the marinade. Place the turkey, skin side up, on the grill rack over the drip pan but not over the preheated coals. Close the grill hood.

5 Grill for 1 to 1¼ hours or until a meat thermometer inserted near the center of the turkey registers 170°. Let the turkey stand for 10 to 15 minutes before slicing. Garnish with fresh thyme, if desired.

TIPS FROM OUR KITCHEN

To check the temperature of the coals: Hold your hand, palm side down, above the coals or drip pan, at the height the food will be cooked. Start counting the seconds, "one thousand one, one thousand two." If you need to remove your hand after three seconds, the coals are medium-hot; after four seconds, they're medium.

If you're starting with a frozen turkey, thaw it in the refrigerator, not on the counter or in a pan of water. Also, be sure that you thoroughly wash the bowl and any utensils that come in contact with the raw turkey before you use the utensils to lift, carry or cut the cooked turkey. *Do not*, under any circumstances, allow the cooked turkey to stand at room temperature for more than two hours. Keep the turkey hot (above 140°) or cold (below 40°).

Nutrition Analysis (*Per Serving*): Calories: 233 / Cholesterol: 85 mg / Carbohydrates: 0 g / Protein: 33 g / Sodium: 90 mg / Fat: 10 g (Saturated Fat: 3 g) / Potassium: 334 mg.

GRILLED TURKEY BREAST

TURKEY FILLET KABOBS

44

Turkey Fillet Kabobs

Makes 4 Servings

1 pound turkey breast tenderloin *or* 1 pound skinless, boneless chicken breast halves
¼ cup soy sauce
¼ cup cooking oil
2 tablespoons honey
1 teaspoon ground ginger
1 teaspoon dry mustard
1 clove garlic, minced
1 green sweet pepper, cut into 1-inch pieces
8 pearl onions, peeled
8 medium whole mushrooms
8 cherry tomatoes
2 cups hot, cooked rice

✦   ✦   ✦

In order to raise funds for scholarships and to purchase books and supplies for the Religious Education Program, St. Joan of Arc Catholic Church members decided to put together a cookbook in which "everyone could take a little ownership." The children involved in the program—preschool through high school—were asked to submit their favorite family recipes. Here is Travis Bode's favorite, Turkey Fillet Kabobs.

Travis Bode
Sharing Family Fare
St. Joan of Arc Catholic Church
Phoenix
ARIZONA

1 Rinse the turkey or chicken and pat dry with paper towels. Cut the turkey into 1-inch cubes or cut the chicken into 2-inch strips that can be folded to form 1-inch pieces.

2 In a small bowl, stir together the soy sauce, cooking oil, honey, ginger, dry mustard and garlic. Add the turkey or chicken, stirring to coat all sides. Marinate at room temperature for 30 minutes or cover and refrigerate overnight.

3 Drain, reserving the marinade. On four 15-inch skewers, alternately thread the turkey or poultry pieces with the peppers, onions and mushrooms. Place on an unheated broiler pan.

4 Broil the kabobs 3 to 4 inches from the heat for 6 minutes, brushing occasionally with the marinade. Turn the kabobs and brush on more marinade. Broil 6 to 8 minutes more or until no pink remains in the center of the turkey or chicken pieces. Add the cherry tomatoes to the ends of the skewers during the last 1 to 2 minutes of broiling to heat them through. Serve the kabobs with the hot, cooked rice.

 Tips from Our Kitchen

Precooking the pearl onions makes peeling them easier. Place the onions in a pan of boiling water for 3 to 4 minutes. Drain. Trim off the root ends and gently press to slip off the skins.

Leave at least ¼-inch space between the meat and vegetables on the skewers so that all the pieces can cook evenly.

Soy sauce is a salty, brown liquid commercially made from fermented soybeans, wheat, water and salt. Many varieties of both Chinese and Japanese soy sauce are available. Soy sauce ranges in color from light to dark, in taste from sweet to extremely salty, and in texture from thin to very thick. If you prefer a less salty flavor or are concerned about your sodium intake, you may prefer to use a low-sodium or reduced-sodium soy sauce in this marinade.

If you use wooden skewers, soak them in water for a few minutes before threading on the meat and vegetables. This will prevent the skewers from burning under the broiler.

Nutrition Analysis (*Per Serving*): Calories: 412 / Cholesterol: 50 mg / Carbohydrates: 46 g / Protein: 27 g / Sodium: 827 mg / Fat: 13 g (Saturated Fat: 2 g) / Potassium: 582 mg.

TURKEY FORESTER

Makes 6 Servings

1½	pounds turkey breast tenderloin steaks
1	clove garlic, halved
¼	cup all-purpose flour
¼	cup butter *or* margarine
8	ounces fresh mushrooms, sliced (3 cups)
⅓	cup dry vermouth
¼	teaspoon salt
⅛	teaspoon pepper
1	teaspoon lemon juice
2	tablespoons snipped parsley

◆ ◆ ◆

Janet Richards adapted one of her mother's recipes to create Turkey Forester. She tells us that much of the conversation when she was growing up centered around food. Now a busy mother of three, she likes this particular recipe for its delicious taste and quick preparation time. Janet says that it is so easy that she is able to prepare the dish while visiting with friends in her kitchen.

Janet Richards
Food For Thought
St. Mary Magdalen
Catholic Church
Council of Catholic Women
St. Eamon's Circle
Alamonte Springs
FLORIDA

1 Rub the turkey steaks with the cut side of the garlic. Discard the garlic.

2 Place the flour in a pie plate or dish with raised sides. Roll each of the turkey steaks in the flour.

3 In a large skillet melt the butter or margarine. Add the turkey steaks to the skillet and cook over medium heat for 1 to 2 minutes per side or until browned.

4 Add the mushrooms, dry vermouth, salt and pepper to the skillet. Cover and simmer about 20 minutes or until the turkey is tender and no longer pink.

5 Transfer the turkey steaks and mushroom mixture to a warm serving dish. Sprinkle with the lemon juice and parsley. Serve immediately.

 TIPS FROM OUR KITCHEN

If you don't have dry vermouth on hand, substitute any dry white wine.

Nutrition Analysis *(Per Serving)*: Calories: 220 / Cholesterol: 70 mg / Carbohydrates: 6 g / Protein: 23 g / Sodium: 215 mg / Fat: 10 g (Saturated Fat: 6 g) / Potassium: 385 mg.

TURKEY FORESTER

TURKEY SCALOPPINE WITH PARMESAN CHEESE

TURKEY SCALOPPINE WITH PARMESAN CHEESE

Makes 4 Servings

4	3-ounce turkey breast slices, ¼ inch thick
¼	cup all-purpose flour
⅛	teaspoon salt
⅛	teaspoon pepper
1	egg
2	tablespoons water
1	cup fresh bread crumbs
½	cup freshly grated Parmesan cheese
¼	cup butter *or* margarine

Snipped parsley

◆　　◆　　◆

St. Thomas's Church parishoners are active in "The Country Cooks," a program in which participants provide large numbers of meals each week to Paul's Place, an urban soup kitchen located in Baltimore. Proceeds from the sale of Two and Company *help to support this program, as well as to provide funding for maintenance of the historic church and its grounds.*

Susan D. Baxter

Two and Company

St. Thomas's Church, Garrison

Forest

Owing Mills

MARYLAND

1 Rinse the turkey slices and pat them dry.

2 Stir together the flour, salt and pepper in a shallow dish.

3 In a second shallow dish, beat together the egg and water.

4 In a third shallow dish, combine the fresh bread crumbs and Parmesan cheese. Dip each turkey slice first in the flour mixture, next in the egg mixture and finally in the bread crumb mixture.

5 In a 12-inch skillet over medium-high heat, melt the butter or margarine. Add the coated turkey slices to the skillet and cook for 2 to 3 minutes on each side or until no pink remains. Transfer the turkey to a serving platter. Garnish with the snipped parsley.

TIPS FROM OUR KITCHEN

To flatten turkey slices to ¼-inch thickness: Wrap each turkey slice in heavy-duty plastic wrap and pound from the center outward with a meat mallet or other heavy utensil.

Fresh Parmesan cheese varies in flavor from mild to robust depending on how long the cheese has been aged. To grate your own Parmesan, use a food processor or hand grater. If you use shaker-ready grated Parmesan cheese, you'll want to use less than the amount called for in the recipe. Close the shaker after each use and store in a cool, dry place.

Use a skillet with a non-stick coating to prevent the cheese from sticking to the skillet.

Nutrition Analysis (*Per Serving*): Calories: 261 / Cholesterol: 90 mg / Carbohydrates: 11 g / Protein: 19 g / Sodium: 309 mg / Fat: 15 g (Saturated Fat: 3 g) / Potassium: 211 mg.

TURKEY LOAF

1 egg, slightly beaten
1 cup herb-seasoned stuffing mix
2 stalks celery, finely chopped
2 large carrots, shredded
1 small onion, finely chopped
¼ cup snipped parsley
2 medium cloves garlic, minced
¼ teaspoon poultry seasoning *or*
  1 teaspoon Worcestershire sauce
⅛ teaspoon pepper
1 pound ground turkey

♦ ♦ ♦

Ellen Robbins is concerned about good nutrition, low cholesterol and dietary restrictions, and she finds that Turkey Loaf is an excellent way to alleviate these concerns. She chose to submit this recipe to Our Best Recipes to You, Again *because it was a little different, and she hoped to encourage the cookbook committee of the High Street United Methodist Church to "focus on healthy eating."*

Ellen Robbins
Our Best Recipes To You, Again
High Street United Methodist
Church
Muncie
INDIANA

1 Preheat the oven to 350°.

2 In a large bowl, stir together the slightly beaten egg, herb-seasoned stuffing mix, celery, carrots, onion, parsley, garlic, poultry seasoning or Worcestershire sauce and pepper. Add the ground turkey; mix thoroughly.

3 Spoon the turkey mixture into an 8x4x2-inch loaf pan; lightly pack down the turkey mixture. Bake in the 350° oven for 40 to 45 minutes or until the turkey loaf is no longer pink and cooked to an internal temperature of 170°.

Place the pan on a wire rack and let the turkey loaf stand for 10 minutes. Remove the turkey loaf from the pan and slice to serve.

 TIPS FROM OUR KITCHEN

You can substitute crushed croutons for the herb-seasoned stuffing mix. To crush the croutons, place them in a heavy plastic bag and flatten them with a rolling pin.

To snip the parsley, place it in a 1-cup glass measure and snip with kitchen shears.

For the best flavor and texture, the vegetables should be chopped into very small pieces before adding them to the ground turkey. To finely chop the celery, cut it into thin lengthwise strips, then thinly slice.

Use an instant-read meat thermometer to check the doneness of the turkey loaf.

Nutrition Analysis (*Per Serving*): Calories: 243 / Cholesterol: 95 mg / Carbohydrates: 18 g / Protein: 19 g / Sodium: 385 mg / Fat: 10 g (Saturated Fat: 3 g) / Potassium: 403 mg.

TURKEY LOAF

OUR FAVORITE HONEY-GLAZED DUCK

OUR FAVORITE HONEY-GLAZED DUCK

Makes 6 to 8 Servings
- 2 medium onions, chopped
- 2 cloves garlic, minced
- ½ cup honey
- ½ cup dry sherry
- ¼ cup soy sauce
- Dash hot pepper sauce
- ½ teaspoon ground ginger
- ¼ teaspoon pepper
- 2 3- to 5-pound domestic ducklings
- Peel of 2 oranges

◆ ◆ ◆

Lynn and John Howard have served Our Favorite Honey-Glazed Duck to many of their dinner guests. Lynn says she likes the simple preparation and suggests that wild rice and a green salad make perfect accompaniments.

Lynn Howard
CordonBlueGrass
Junior League of Louisville, Inc.
Louisville
KENTUCKY

1 In a blender or food processor, thoroughly blend or process the onions, garlic, honey, sherry, soy sauce, hot pepper sauce, ginger and pepper until liquified. Set aside.

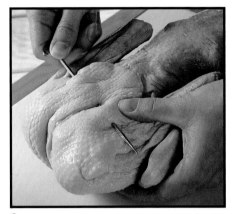

2 Preheat oven to 350°. Rinse each duckling and wipe inside and out with paper towels. Skewer the neck skin to the back and tie the legs to the tail. Snip off the wing tips and twist the wings under the back.

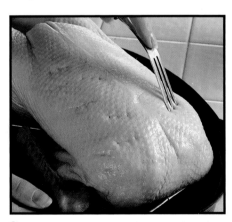

3 Place the ducklings, breast sides up, on a rack in a roasting pan. Prick the breast skin. Insert a meat thermometer into the center of one of the inside thigh muscles. Place the orange peel in the pan below the ducks.

4 Roast the ducks in the 350° oven for 2 to 2½ hours or until the meat thermometer registers 180°. Baste the ducks generously with the glaze after 1½ hours and then every 15 minutes until done.

TIPS FROM OUR KITCHEN

To serve three or four people, halve this recipe.

Don't brush the ducklings with the glaze too soon or it will burn before the birds are done.

If you do not have a meat thermometer, cook the ducklings until the drumsticks move easily in their sockets and the duck is no longer pink.

For a holiday meal, try serving this duck with mashed sweet potatoes and whole cranberry sauce. A few orange slices will make a colorful garnish.

Nutrition Analysis *(Per Serving)*: Calories: 799 / Cholesterol: 165 mg / Carbohydrates: 29 g / Protein: 39 g / Sodium: 806 mg / Fat: 56 g (Saturated Fat: 19 g) / Potassium: 517 mg.

meat

Nothing satisfies a hearty appetite like meat. The vigorous eaters in your house will relish Stuffed Flank Steak or Pork Tenderloin-Mushroom Casserole. For those who delight in ethnically inspired cuisine, Sweet-and-Sour Pork, Beef Stroganoff, and Veal Parmigiana offer a world of flavor. Prune-Stuffed Roast Pork or Filets in Cognac Cream Sauce will impress even the most fastidious gourmet in your family. Whether you're in the mood for simple and filling, such as Stuffed Cabbage, or culinary splendor, such as Veal Rolls with Rice Piedmont, you're guaranteed to find a pleasing meal in this chapter.

STUFFED FLANK STEAK

STUFFED FLANK STEAK

Makes 6 to 8 Servings
- 1 1½- to 2-pound beef flank steak
- Salt
- Pepper
- ¼ teaspoon dried marjoram, crushed
- ¼ teaspoon dried basil, crushed
- ¼ teaspoon dried parsley flakes
- 8 ounces fresh mushrooms, sliced
- 2 green onions, thinly sliced (¼ cup)
- 2 tablespoons butter *or* margarine
- ½ cup soft bread crumbs
- 2 tablespoons butter *or* margarine, melted
- 2 tablespoons Worcestershire sauce

◆ ◆ ◆

Judy Chambers told us that Stuffed Flank Steak is a family favorite. She gave the recipe to her daughter, who passed it along to some of her friends. Judy emphasizes that when you cook Stuffed Flank Steak, you should be sure to keep basting for a tender, flavorful steak.

Judy Chambers
VIP Cookbook: A Potpourri of Virginia Cooking
The American Cancer Society, Virginia Division
Vienna
VIRGINIA

1 Preheat the oven to 425°.

2 Pound the steak to a ¼-inch thickness. (It should be approximately a 12x8-inch rectangle.) Sprinkle the steak lightly with salt and pepper. Rub the marjoram, basil and parsley on 1 side of the meat.

3 Cook the mushrooms and onions in the 2 tablespoons butter or margarine until tender. Stir in the bread crumbs.

4 Spread the mushroom mixture over the herbs on the steak to within 1 inch of the edges.

5 Roll up the steak, jelly-roll fashion, starting from a short side. Tie with a string. Place the meat, seam side down, on a rack in a roasting pan. Stir together the 2 tablespoons melted butter or margarine and the Worcestershire sauce; brush over the steak.

6 Bake in the 425° oven for 45 to 60 minutes or until the meat is tender, brushing occasionally with the butter-Worcestershire sauce mixture. Remove the strings; slice and serve.

 TIPS FROM OUR KITCHEN

When pounding the meat, first cover the steak with heavy-duty plastic wrap; lightweight plastic wrap or waxed paper is likely to tear as you pound. Pound from the center outward until the meat reaches the desired thickness.

If fresh marjoram, basil and parsley are available, use ¾ teaspoon of each instead of the dried herbs.

If you prefer your meat with gravy, serve this dish with bottled gravy or gravy prepared from a packaged mix.

The steak can be served with potatoes or rice. Or, for something a little different, try serving it with spinach noodles or orzo.

Nutrition Analysis (*Per Serving*): Calories: 257 / Cholesterol: 74 mg / Carbohydrates: 4 g / Protein: 23 g / Sodium: 247 mg / Fat: 16 g (Saturated Fat: 8 g) / Potassium: 493 mg.

FILETS IN COGNAC CREAM SAUCE

4 5-ounce beef tenderloin
   steaks (1-inch thick)
⅛ teaspoon freshly ground
   black pepper
½ cup cognac
3 tablespoons butter *or*
   margarine
1 tablespoon olive oil *or*
   cooking oil
2 shallots, finely
   chopped (¼ cup)
½ cup heavy whipping cream
½ teaspoon lemon juice

❖ ❖ ❖

*David Panek's love of cooking
and willingness to experiment led
him to develop a recipe for
Cognac Cream Sauce. Successive
alterations produced this superb
recipe for Filets in Cognac Cream
Sauce, which he suggests you serve
with a good California red wine.
We suggest you try this recipe the
next time you have something
to celebrate.*

David Panek
<u>What's Cooking with</u>
<u>Harvey's Employees</u>
Stateline
NEVADA

1 Sprinkle the steaks with the pepper.
Place the steaks in a plastic bag and set
the open bag in a deep bowl. Pour *¼
cup* of the cognac over the steaks. Seal
the bag. Marinate at room temperature
for 30 minutes. Drain the steaks, then
pat dry with paper towels.

2 In a large skillet, heat *1 tablespoon* of
the butter or margarine and the olive
oil. Brown the steaks for 2 minutes per
side.

3 Reduce the heat to medium-low and
cook about 6 minutes for rare doneness
(8 minutes for medium-rare), turning
once. Remove the steaks to a platter
and cover to keep warm.

4 Drain the fat from the skillet. Melt
the remaining butter or margarine; add
the shallots and cook over low heat for
1 minute. Pour in the remaining
cognac and heat to boiling. Boil gently
about 1 minute or until the liquid is
reduced by half.

5 Add the cream; boil about 3 minutes
more or until the liquid is once again
reduced by half. Add the lemon juice.
Spoon the sauce over the steaks.

 TIPS FROM OUR KITCHEN

If you'd like to conserve your cognac,
save the ¼ cup that's used to marinate
the meat and add it to the skillet after
you've cooked the shallots.

If you prefer, you can substitute beef
top sirloin steak for the beef tenderloin
in this recipe.

Nutrition Analysis (*Per Serving*): Calories: 444 / Cholesterol: 144 mg / Carbohydrates: 3 g /
Protein: 28 g / Sodium: 159 mg / Fat: 32 g (Saturated Fat: 16 g) / Potassium: 460 mg.

FILETS IN COGNAC CREAM SAUCE

PEPPERED CHUTNEY ROAST

PEPPERED CHUTNEY ROAST

Makes 8 to 12 Servings

Marinade:

½ cup unsweetened pineapple juice
⅓ cup steak sauce
¼ cup Worcestershire sauce
¼ cup port wine
3 tablespoons lemon juice
1½ teaspoons seasoned salt
¾ teaspoon pepper
¾ teaspoon lemon pepper seasoning
¾ teaspoon dry mustard

Roast:

1 2- to 3-pound beef tenderloin
1 teaspoon cracked black pepper
4 slices bacon
¼ cup chutney, snipped
Chutney (optional)

◆　◆　◆

Every other year, the Independence Regional Health Center Auxiliary hosts a garden tour during which packed lunches are sold. Frequent requests for recipes used in the lunches inspired Bouquet Garni. *Profits from cookbook sales help benefit the Cliffview Center for Women's Health.*

Brenda Lewis
Bouquet Garni
Independence Regional Health
Center Auxiliary
Independence
MISSOURI

1 To make the marinade: Stir together the pineapple juice, steak sauce, Worcestershire sauce, port wine, lemon juice, seasoned salt, pepper, lemon pepper seasoning and dry mustard.

2 To prepare the roast: Place the tenderloin in a large plastic bag. Pour the marinade over the meat and close the bag. Place the bag in a shallow baking dish. Refrigerate for 6 to 24 hours, turning the meat occasionally to distribute the marinade evenly. Drain the meat, reserving the marinade.

3 Preheat the oven to 425°. Sprinkle the meat with the cracked black pepper. Place the meat on a rack in a shallow roasting pan and arrange the bacon slices over the top.

4 Roast the meat, uncovered, in the 425° oven for 35 to 45 minutes or until a meat thermometer registers 135°. Baste the meat twice with the reserved marinade during roasting.

5 Remove the bacon slices from the meat and spoon the chutney evenly over the roast. Roast for 5 to 10 minutes more or until the meat thermometer registers 140° for rare.

6 Using 2 spatulas, transfer the roast to a serving platter and allow it to stand 10 minutes before slicing. Serve with additional chutney, if desired.

TIPS FROM OUR KITCHEN

This marinade also works well with beef eye of round, boneless beef sirloin roast, beef tip roast, or 2 pork tenderloins. For these cuts, use a lower oven temperature (325°) and a meat thermometer. Allow 2 to 3 hours for the beef roasts to reach 160° (medium). Cook the pork tenderloin to 160° (medium well); start checking after 45 minutes.

Placing the bacon strips over the tenderloin is an example of *larding*. It's done to make the meat juicier and more flavorful.

You can purchase cracked black pepper, or crack the whole peppercorns yourself using a mortar and pestle.

Chutney is an East Indian specialty made from fruits or vegetables. It can range in texture from smooth to chunky, and in flavor from sweet to tart to spicy-hot.

Nutrition Analysis (*Per Serving*): Calories: 157 / Cholesterol: 44 mg / Carbohydrates: 8 g / Protein: 15 g / Sodium: 460 mg / Fat: 6 g (Saturated Fat: 2 g) / Potassium: 304 mg.

HERBED MUSHROOM POT ROAST

Makes 8 to 10 Servings

3 tablespoons all-purpose flour
1 3- to 4-pound beef pot roast
2 tablespoons cooking oil
½ teaspoon salt
¼ teaspoon pepper
1 medium onion, sliced
½ cup water
⅓ cup dry cooking sherry
¼ cup catsup
¼ teaspoon dry mustard
¼ teaspoon dried marjoram, crushed
¼ teaspoon dried rosemary, crushed
¼ teaspoon dried thyme, crushed
1 small bay leaf
1 6-ounce can whole mushrooms
¼ cup cold water
2 tablespoons cornstarch

❖ ❖ ❖

The Buncombe County Extension Homemakers Association is a volunteer organization that helps improve "the quality of life in the family, home and community," through education, community outreach and leadership development. Cookbook profits are used to support the association's educational projects.

Cookbook Committee
Heart of the Mountains
Buncombe County Extension Homemakers Association
Ashville
NORTH CAROLINA

1 Sprinkle the flour over both sides of the roast.

2 In a Dutch oven, heat the cooking oil. Transfer the meat to the Dutch oven and brown slowly on all sides. Season with the salt and pepper. Add the onion slices.

3 In a large bowl, stir together the ½ cup water, the sherry, catsup, dry mustard, marjoram, rosemary, thyme and bay leaf. Carefully add the mixture to the Dutch oven. Cover and cook over low heat for 2 to 2½ hours or until the meat is tender.

4 Add the *undrained* mushrooms; heat through.

5 Transfer the meat to a serving platter. Remove the bay leaf from the cooking liquid and discard.

6 Stir together the ¼ cup cold water and the cornstarch. Add the water-cornstarch mixture to the cooking liquid. Cook and stir until thickened and bubbly. Cook and stir for 2 minutes more. Serve with the meat.

TIPS FROM OUR KITCHEN

We recommend using a beef chuck arm or a blade roast for the beef pot roast in this recipe.

Coating the meat with the flour helps to increase browning and adds flavor. To coat the meat: Pat the roast dry, then sprinkle the flour evenly over the meat. Shake or pat the roast until all of the surfaces are coated.

If you have fresh herbs, use ¾ teaspoon of each in place of the dried herbs in this recipe.

Nutrition Analysis (*Per Serving*): Calories: 350 / Cholesterol: 124 mg / Carbohydrates: 8 g / Protein: 41 g / Sodium: 407 mg / Fat: 16 g (Saturated Fat: 5 g) / Potassium: 443 mg.

HERBED MUSHROOM POT ROAST

BEEF BURGUNDY WITH RICE

BEEF BURGUNDY WITH RICE

Makes 6 to 8 Servings

- 5 medium onions, thinly sliced (3 cups)
- 2 tablespoons cooking oil
- 2 pounds boneless beef chuck, cut into 1½-inch cubes
- 3 tablespoons all-purpose flour
- ½ teaspoon salt
- ½ teaspoon dried thyme, crushed
- ½ teaspoon dried marjoram, crushed
- ¼ teaspoon pepper
- 1 cup dry red wine
- ½ cup beef broth
- 8 ounces fresh mushrooms, sliced (3 cups)
- 4 cups hot cooked rice

♦ ♦ ♦

When we called Myke Brehm Gerrish, she was in the process of preparing a dinner for 17 family members. Fortunately, she had time to talk with us about her recipe for Beef Burgundy with Rice. Although it's been a while since she's prepared this dish—they don't eat as much beef anymore—Myke remembered that this is a hearty, robust meal that's great for company.

Myke Brehm Gerrish
<u>10,000 Tastes of Minnesota</u>
The Women's Club of Minneapolis
Minneapolis
MINNESOTA

1 In a 4-quart Dutch oven or large heavy skillet, cook the onions in the cooking oil until golden. Remove the onions from the Dutch oven or skillet; set aside.

2 Add the beef cubes, *half* at a time, to the Dutch oven or skillet; cook until the beef is browned. Return all of the meat to the Dutch oven or skillet.

3 In a small bowl, stir together the flour, salt, thyme, marjoram and pepper. Sprinkle the seasonings over the beef in the skillet, stirring the beef cubes to coat.

4 Carefully add the red wine and beef broth to the beef mixture. Cook and stir until the mixture is bubbly. Reduce heat; cover and simmer about 1½ hours or until the beef is nearly tender. Return the onions to the Dutch oven or skillet. Stir in the mushrooms. Cover and cook about 20 minutes more or until the beef is tender.

5 Serve the beef mixture with the hot cooked rice.

 TIPS FROM OUR KITCHEN

Browning only half of the beef cubes at a time will help ensure that they are browned and not stewed.

When preparing fresh mushrooms, do not soak them in water; soaking makes them soggy and ruins their texture. Instead, wipe the mushrooms with a clean, damp cloth or lightly rinse them under cool running water and dry them with paper towels.

Nutrition Analysis (*Per Serving*): Calories: 565 / Cholesterol: 110 mg / Carbohydrates: 54 g / Protein: 42 g / Sodium: 347 mg / Fat: 16 g (Saturated Fat: 5 g) / Potassium: 736 mg.

BEEF STROGANOFF

Makes 6 Servings

1 pound beef round steak, cut into ¾-inch cubes
½ teaspoon paprika
¼ teaspoon salt
¼ teaspoon pepper
⅛ teaspoon garlic salt
¼ cup margarine *or* butter
1 small onion, chopped
1½ cups sliced fresh mushrooms
¾ cup beef broth
1 small bay leaf
2 teaspoons Worcestershire sauce
2 tablespoons all-purpose flour
1 8-ounce carton dairy sour cream
1 8-ounce package medium noodles, cooked (4½ cups dry noodles)

◆ ◆ ◆

Members of the Christian Women's Fellowship sell craft items and hold food sales at which they promote the sale of their fund-raising cookbook. These efforts contribute to the church's many outreach programs.

Diane Wright
<u>*First Christian Church Centennial*</u>
<u>*Commemorative Cookbook*</u>
First Christian Church
(Disciples of Christ)
Herington
KANSAS

1 Season the meat with the paprika, salt, pepper and garlic salt.

2 In a large skillet over medium-high heat, melt the margarine or butter. Add the meat and onion. Cook and stir until the meat is browned on all sides.

3 Add the mushrooms, beef broth, bay leaf and Worcestershire sauce to the skillet. Bring to a boil. Reduce heat, cover and simmer for 1 to 1¼ hours or until the meat is tender. Remove and discard the bay leaf.

4 In a small bowl, stir together the flour and sour cream. Add the sour cream mixture to the meat mixture in the skillet. Cook and stir over medium heat until the sauce is thickened and bubbly. Cook and stir for 1 minute more. Serve over the hot cooked noodles.

 TIPS FROM OUR KITCHEN

To season the meat cubes evenly, place the paprika, salt, pepper and garlic salt in a heavy plastic bag. Add the meat cubes and shake.

Sour cream that is tightly covered will keep in the refrigerator up to four weeks. Freezing is not recommended because the sour cream will separate as it thaws. If you notice any spots of mold on the surface of refrigerated sour cream, discard the entire container.

In this recipe, the sour cream is mixed with the flour before it is added to the skillet to prevent it from curdling when it is heated.

To reduce fat and calories, you can substitute "light" sour cream for the regular sour cream in the recipe.

Nutrition Analysis (*Per Serving*): Calories: 426 / Cholesterol: 65 mg / Carbohydrates: 35 g / Protein: 25 g / Sodium: 392 mg / Fat: 20 g (Saturated Fat: 8 g) / Potassium: 461 mg.

BEEF STROGANOFF

SWISS BLISS

Swiss Bliss

Makes 8 Servings
- 2 pounds boneless beef chuck arm pot roast
- 1 envelope onion soup mix
- 3 cups sliced fresh mushrooms
- 1 medium green sweet pepper, cut into thin strips
- 1 16- ounce can tomatoes, drained (reserve juice) and cut up
- ¼ teaspoon pepper
- 1 tablespoon cornstarch
- 1 tablespoon steak sauce
- Snipped parsley (optional)

◆　　◆　　◆

Jan Kormann told us that she received this scrumptious recipe for Swiss Bliss back in the early 1950s. "It's a wonderful recipe for family and friends." Jan made the dish often for her family; now that her children are all grown, however, she finds that she mostly makes Swiss Bliss when she is entertaining. Jan adds green sweet pepper to the ingredients for both flavor and color.

Jan Kormann
<u>Immanuel Lutheran Church</u>
<u>Cookbook</u>
Immanuel Lutheran Ladies Aid
Immanuel Lutheran Church
Michigan City
INDIANA

1 Preheat the oven to 375°.

2 Cut a 48x18-inch piece of heavy-duty aluminum foil. Fold the aluminum foil in half to form a 24x18-inch rectangle. Place on a 15x10x1-inch baking pan.

3 Cut the beef roast into 4 portions. Arrange the beef in the center of the aluminum foil.

4 Sprinkle the onion soup mix, mushrooms, green sweet pepper and tomatoes over the beef. Sprinkle the pepper over all.

5 In a small bowl, stir together the reserved tomato juice, cornstarch and steak sauce. Pour the mixture over the beef and vegetables. Bring the edges of the aluminum foil up and over the beef and vegetables; double-fold the aluminum foil edges together to seal the packet tightly.

6 Bake in the 375° oven for 2 hours. To serve, very carefully open the aluminum foil packet. Place the beef and vegetables on a serving platter. If desired, sprinkle with the parsley.

 Tips from Our Kitchen

Since the beef juices can't drain, look for a roast that has little fat and be sure to trim any surface fat.

If desired, bake potatoes alongside the beef packet or serve the beef with mashed potatoes, cooked rice, barley or noodles.

Nutrition Analysis (*Per Serving*): Calories: 206 / Cholesterol: 72 mg / Carbohydrates: 8 g / Protein: 25 g / Sodium: 610 mg / Fat: 8 g (Saturated Fat: 3 g) / Potassium: 478 mg.

GIANT STUFFED SHELLS

Makes 5 to 6 Servings

6	ounces giant pasta shells (about 20)
1	pound ground beef
1	large onion, chopped (1 cup)
1	clove garlic, minced
2	cups shredded mozzarella cheese (8 ounces)
1	egg, beaten
½	cup fine dry Italian-style *or* seasoned bread crumbs
¼	teaspoon pepper
1	27- to 30-ounce jar spaghetti sauce
¼	cup grated Parmesan cheese

❖ ❖ ❖

Nancy Brix submitted Giant Stuffed Shells to the <u>Mark Twain Library Cookbook</u> *not only to share the recipe, but also because she has recipes hidden everywhere and by submitting this one to the cookbook, she would "know where to find it!" When Nancy makes this recipe for company, she always makes extra because her family loves it. And occasionally she makes the shells without meat for her daughter's friends who are vegetarians.*

Nancy Brix
<u>*Mark Twain Library Cookbook*</u>
The Mark Twain Library
Association
Redding
CONNECTICUT

1 Preheat the oven to 400°.

2 Cook the pasta shells in *boiling water* according to the package directions; drain. Rinse the shells with *cold water* and drain again. Set the shells aside.

3 Meanwhile, in a large skillet over medium heat, cook the ground beef, onion and garlic until the meat is browned. Remove from heat; drain the fat from the skillet. Stir in the mozzarella cheese, beaten egg, bread crumbs and pepper.

4 Spoon about *3 tablespoons* of the meat mixture into *each* pasta shell.

5 Pour about *¾ cup* of the spaghetti sauce into the bottom of a 3-quart rectangular baking dish. Arrange the stuffed shells over the sauce in the dish. Pour the remaining sauce over the shells. Sprinkle with the Parmesan cheese.

6 Loosely cover the baking dish with aluminum foil. Bake in the 400° oven for 20 to 25 minutes or until heated through. Garnish with fresh parsley, if desired.

TIPS FROM OUR KITCHEN

Giant pasta shells are also known as *conchiglioni*. Cook them just until tender because overcooking the shells increases the chance that they'll break when you spoon in the meat filling.

For a spicier filling, you can use half ground beef or ground turkey and half Italian sausage in place of the ground beef.

Turn this dish into a make-ahead dinner by completely cooling the cooked meat mixture and shells before filling them. Then, layer the filled shells with the sauce as directed; cover the baking dish and refrigerate. Bake in a 375° oven for 35 to 40 minutes. Uncover the dish and bake for 15 to 20 minutes more or until heated through.

Nutrition Analysis (*Per Serving*): Calories: 652 / Cholesterol: 128 mg / Carbohydrates: 53 g / Protein: 40 g / Sodium: 1500 mg / Fat: 31 g (Saturated Fat: 11 g) / Potassium: 1044 mg.

GIANT STUFFED SHELLS

STUFFED CABBAGE

STUFFED CABBAGE

Makes 6 Servings

- 1 large head cabbage
- 1 pound ground beef, ground pork *or* ground turkey
- 1 8-ounce can stewed tomatoes
- ⅓ cup uncooked long grain rice
- ⅓ cup chopped onion
- 1 egg, beaten
- ¼ teaspoon salt
- ⅛ teaspoon garlic powder
- ⅛ teaspoon pepper
- 1 15-ounce can tomato sauce
- 1 10¾-ounce can condensed tomato soup

◆   ◆   ◆

Laura Routhier often does her own canning, and she uses her own canned tomatoes when making the sauce for Stuffed Cabbage. The recipe suits her whole family—her children enjoy the stuffing, but not the cabbage, whereas her husband loves the whole dish. Laura told us that this is a hearty recipe, which she makes most often in the winter.

Laura Routhier
Laboratory Approved Recipes
Pathology Laboratories Wake
Medical Center
Raleigh
NORTH CAROLINA

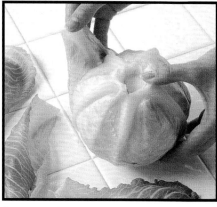

1 Steam the head of cabbage for 8 minutes. Carefully pull off the cabbage leaves. Set aside *12* medium to large cabbage leaves; reserve the remaining cabbage leaves for another use.

2 In a large bowl, stir together the ground beef, pork or turkey, stewed tomatoes, rice, onion, beaten egg, salt, garlic powder and pepper. Stir until all of the ingredients are well mixed.

3 Spoon about ⅓ *cup* of the meat mixture onto the center of *each* cabbage leaf. Fold the long edges of the leaf over the filling. Starting at the short unfolded edge, carefully roll up each leaf.

4 Place the cabbage rolls in a Dutch oven. Stir together the tomato sauce and undiluted tomato soup. Pour the sauce mixture over the cabbage rolls. Bring the mixture to a boil; reduce heat. Cover and simmer about 1 hour or until the meat filling is no longer pink and the rice is tender.

 TIPS FROM OUR KITCHEN

Instead of steaming a whole head of cabbage, you can soften individual cabbage leaves by carefully dipping them into boiling water.

If desired, substitute a can of herbed tomato sauce or just add dried herbs, such as oregano, thyme, marjoram and basil, to the plain tomato sauce.

If you make this dish ahead of time, cover and refrigerate the cabbage rolls. Then, when ready, add an additional 10 to 15 minutes to the cooking time.

Nutrition Analysis (*Per Serving*): Calories: 293 / Cholesterol: 82 mg / Carbohydrates: 30 g / Protein: 20 g / Sodium: 1044 mg / Fat: 11 g (Saturated Fat: 4 g) / Potassium: 971 mg.

COMPANY MEAT LOAF

1	pound lean ground beef
1	pound ground veal
6	saltine crackers, crushed
2	eggs, lightly beaten
2	green onions, finely chopped
½	cups milk
¼	cup snipped parsley
¼	cup finely chopped celery
1	teaspoon soy sauce
1	teaspoon Worcestershire sauce
¼	teaspoon salt
⅛	teaspoon black pepper

Dash of garlic powder

Topping:

¼	cup catsup
3 to 4	slices bacon, slightly cooked

Vegetables:

16 to 24	small red potatoes
1	green sweet pepper, sliced

✦　✦　✦

The Richardson Woman's Club cookbook, The Texas Experience, boasts that it "comes out stoutly for Texas cooking!" This recipe for age-old simple fare, meat loaf, is a perfect example of cooking with imagination and for good taste.

Marge Veerman
The Texas Experience
The Richardson Woman's Club
Richardson
TEXAS

1 Preheat oven to 325°.

2 To make the meat loaf: Combine the beef, veal, crackers, eggs, onions, milk, parsley, celery, soy sauce, Worcestershire sauce, salt, pepper and garlic powder. Add more milk if texture is too stiff.

3 To shape the loaf: Pat meat mixture into an 8x4-inch baking dish, then invert into a shallow baking dish.

4 To make the topping: Cover the top of the meat with the catsup and the bacon slices.

5 To make the vegetables: Surround the meat loaf with the whole potatoes. Cover with foil. Bake in the 325° oven for 1 hour.

6 Uncover; carefully spoon off the drippings in the pan. Add the green sweet pepper on top of the potatoes. Bake in the 325° oven, uncovered, for 30 to 40 minutes or until the meat and potatoes are done.

7 To serve, arrange the meat and vegetables on a platter.

TIPS FROM OUR KITCHEN

Using lean ground beef and precooking the bacon help to lower the fat content in this meat loaf.

To keep the skin on the new potatoes looking pretty, cut a wide strip around the middle of each potato with a sharp knife.

Nutrition Analysis *(Per Serving):* Calories: 338 / Cholesterol: 139mg / Carbohydrates: 32g / Protein: 28g / Sodium: 357 mg / Fat: 11g (Saturated Fat: 4g) / Potassium: 867mg.

COMPANY MEAT LOAF

MANICOTTI CHEESE BAKE

MANICOTTI CHEESE BAKE

Makes 4 Servings
- 8 manicotti shells
- 1 beaten egg
- 2 cups ricotta cheese
- 1 cup shredded mozzarella cheese
- ½ pound ground beef
- ¼ cup finely chopped onion
- ½ teaspoon garlic powder
- 2 cups water
- 1 6-ounce can tomato paste
- 1½ teaspoons dried Italian seasoning
- 1 teaspoon sugar

Salt

Pepper
- ½ cup shredded mozzarella cheese
- ¼ cup grated Parmesan cheese

♦ ♦ ♦

Sister Firminia has been a cook for at least 50 years. Originally from Italy, her specialty is Italian cuisine. Today, Sister Firminia cooks for 30 to 40 sisters at the Apostles of the Sacred Heart of Jesus. She told us that she discovered this recipe for Manicotti Cheese Bake quite awhile ago, and it's so popular that she makes it often.

Sister Firminia
Another Spoonful of Love
Morning Star School
Pinellas Park
FLORIDA

1 Partially cook the manicotti shells in *boiling salted water* for 5 minutes. Drain the shells; set aside.

2 In a large bowl, stir together the beaten egg, ricotta cheese and the 1 cup shredded mozzarella cheese. Using a small spoon, fill *each* manicotti shell with *some* of the cheese mixture.

3 In a medium saucepan over medium-high heat, stir together the ground beef, onion and garlic powder. Cook until the beef is browned; drain the excess fat from the beef mixture.

4 Add the water, tomato paste, Italian seasoning, sugar and salt and pepper to taste. Bring the mixture to a boil; reduce heat and simmer, uncovered, for 1 hour, stirring occasionally.

5 Preheat the oven to 350°. Spoon *half* of the sauce into the bottom of a 2-quart oval baking dish. Place the filled manicotti shells in a single layer over the sauce in the dish. Pour the remaining sauce over the shells.

6 Cover with aluminum foil and bake in the 350° oven for 20 minutes. Remove the aluminum foil and sprinkle the ½ cup shredded mozzarella cheese and the grated Parmesan cheese over the shells and sauce. Bake, uncovered, about 10 minutes more or until heated through.

 TIPS FROM OUR KITCHEN

If you are preparing this recipe ahead of time, cook the sauce and let it cool before combining it with the filled shells in the baking dish. Cover the assembled dish with aluminum foil and refrigerate. Bake, covered, in a 350° oven for 30 to 40 minutes. Then proceed as directed.

If you make this casserole to give away, add a card with the cooking directions and a reminder to keep the casserole refrigerated until ready to bake.

Manicotti shells are large, tube-shaped pasta. The easiest way to fill them is to use a long narrow spoon, such as the type used for feeding babies or for iced tea.

Nutrition Analysis (*Per Serving*): Calories: 605 / Cholesterol: 155 mg / Carbohydrates: 43 g / Protein: 44 g / Sodium: 606 mg / Fat: 28 g (Saturated Fat: 15 g) / Potassium: 786 mg.

CLASSIC SPAGHETTI AND MEATBALLS

Makes 6 Servings

1	egg, slightly beaten
¼	cup water
1	teaspoon salt
½	teaspoon dried basil, crushed
¼	teaspoon pepper
½	cup fine dry bread crumbs
¼	cup grated Parmesan cheese
1½	pounds lean ground beef
1	tablespoon olive oil
1	28-ounce can tomatoes, cut up
1	6-ounce can tomato paste
¼	cup chopped onion
2	tablespoons snipped parsley
2	cloves garlic, minced
1	teaspoon dried oregano, crushed
½	teaspoon salt
¼	teaspoon anise seed, crushed
12	ounces spaghetti, cooked and drained

Grated Parmesan cheese (optional)

❖   ❖   ❖

Patty Squires has had this recipe for Classic Spaghetti and Meatballs for years, and it's an old standby that she makes whenever she's in the mood for spaghetti. Patty added that sometimes she just makes the sauce—without the meatballs—to serve with other dishes.

Patty Squires
Sassafras!
The Junior League of Springfield
Springfield
MISSOURI

1 In a large bowl, stir together the beaten egg, water, the 1 teaspoon salt, the basil and pepper. Stir in the bread crumbs and the ¼ cup Parmesan cheese. Add the ground beef and mix well.

2 Shape the mixture into thirty-six 1-inch meatballs. In a 12-inch skillet, heat the olive oil. Add the meatballs and cook over medium-low heat, turning occasionally, until the meatballs are browned. Drain and discard the excess fat.

3 Meanwhile, in a medium bowl, stir together the *undrained* tomatoes, tomato paste, onion, parsley, garlic, oregano, the ½ teaspoon salt and the anise seed. Add the sauce to the meatballs in the skillet and bring to a boil. Reduce heat and simmer, covered, for 15 minutes. Uncover and simmer about 15 minutes more or until the sauce reaches the desired consistency.

4 Serve the meatballs and sauce over the cooked and drained spaghetti. Serve with additional grated Parmesan cheese, if desired.

TIPS FROM OUR KITCHEN

To make even-size meatballs: Pat the meat mixture into a 6x6-inch square. Make 5 vertical and 5 horizontal cuts. Or, divide the meat mixture into thirds. Shape each third into a 12-inch roll and cut each roll into 12 pieces.

If you prefer, you can brown and bake the meatballs in the oven: Place the meatballs in a single layer in a 15x10x1-inch baking pan. Bake in a 375° oven about 20 minutes or until no pink remains. Drain. Add the meatballs to the sauce after uncovering.

Nutrition Analysis (*Per Serving*): Calories: 584 / Cholesterol: 109 mg / Carbohydrates: 65 g / Protein: 35 g / Sodium: 978 mg / Fat: 20 g (Saturated Fat: 7 g) / Potassium: 941 mg.

CLASSIC SPAGHETTI AND MEATBALLS

CINCINNATI CHILI

CINCINNATI CHILI

Makes 6 to 8 Servings

2	pounds ground beef
2	cups finely chopped onion
4	cups beef stock
2	8-ounce cans tomato sauce
2 to 3	tablespoons chili powder
2	tablespoons cider vinegar
2	teaspoons Worcestershire sauce
½	ounce unsweetened chocolate, grated
2	teaspoons minced garlic
1	teaspoon ground cinnamon
1	teaspoon ground cumin
½	teaspoon salt
½	teaspoon ground red pepper
¼	teaspoon ground allspice
¼	teaspoon ground cloves
1	bay leaf
12	ounces spaghetti, cooked and drained

◆   ◆   ◆

Chili from Cincinnati? Yes! It's as much a ritual there as gumbo is in New Orleans or steak sandwiches are in Philadelphia. This particular version was brought from Ohio to Alaska by Rabbi Gerald J. Klein, a military rabbi stationed in Anchorage.

Rabbi Gerald J. Klein
<u>*Heaven Scent:*</u>
<u>*An Alaskan Jewish Cookbook*</u>
Anchorage
ALASKA

1 In a 4-quart Dutch oven, cook the beef and onion for 10 minutes or until the meat is browned, stirring often. Drain the excess fat. Add the beef stock and simmer, uncovered, for 10 minutes.

2 Stir the tomato sauce into the beef mixture. Then add the chili powder, vinegar, Worcestershire sauce, chocolate, garlic, cinnamon, cumin, salt, red pepper, allspice, cloves and bay leaf. Simmer the mixture, uncovered, for 1 hour, stirring occasionally.

3 Remove the bay leaf. Skim off any excess fat from the sauce. Serve the chili over the hot cooked spaghetti.

 TIPS FROM OUR KITCHEN

To grate chocolate, rub a cool, firm square of chocolate across a grater. The finer the grater, the smaller the chocolate pieces will be and the more evenly the chocolate will be distributed in the chili.

To keep this chili from getting greasy, drain the cooked ground beef in a colander, then pat it with paper toweling to absorb the excess fat before combining it with the other ingredients.

For a traditional presentation, serve this chili over the spaghetti and then top it with a generous amount of shredded cheddar cheese. If you wish, garnish it with a jalapeno pepper and fresh cilantro.

Nutrition Analysis (*Per Serving*): Calories: 610 / Cholesterol: 95 mg / Carbohydrates: 72 g / Protein: 44 g / Sodium: 1,378 mg / Fat: 18 g / (Saturated Fat: 6 g) / Potassium: 1,008 mg.

VEAL ROLLS WITH RICE PIEDMONT

Makes 8 Servings
Veal Rolls:
- ¼ cup snipped parsley
- 1½ teaspoons dried rosemary, crushed
- 1 teaspoon minced garlic
- ¼ teaspoon pepper
- 8 4-ounce veal scallopini *or* turkey steaks, pounded to ⅛-inch thickness
- 4 ounces very thinly sliced prosciutto *or* ham
- 2 tablespoons olive oil
- ½ cup dry Marsala *or* dry sherry
- 4 cups sliced fresh mushrooms

Rice Piedmont:
- 4 cups hot cooked rice
- 2 cups fresh *or* frozen peas, cooked
- ¼ cup butter *or* margarine, melted
- Dash ground nutmeg
- ¾ cup grated Parmesan cheese

◆　　◆　　◆

Rollini Di Vitella (veal rolls) with Rice Piedmont comes to us from Eugene, Oregon. This delicious version of the classic Italian dish is representative of the rich cultural diversity of the Oregon people.

<u>A Taste of Oregon</u>
The Junior League of Eugene
Eugene
OREGON

1 To make the rolls: In a small bowl, combine the parsley, rosemary, garlic and pepper. Lay the veal scallopini or turkey steaks on a flat surface. Sprinkle about *1½ teaspoons* of the herb mixture on *each* scallopini or turkey steak. Then top *each* scallopini or turkey steak with the prosciutto or ham, dividing it equally.

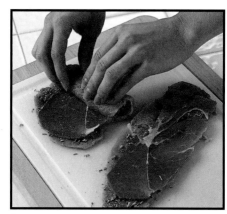

2 Starting from a short side, roll up each veal scallopini or turkey steak.

3 Fasten each veal or turkey roll with a wooden toothpick.

4 In a large skillet, quickly cook *half* of the veal or turkey rolls in *1 tablespoon* of the oil, lightly browning the rolls on all sides. Remove the rolls to a plate as they brown. Repeat with the remaining rolls and oil.

5 Remove the skillet from the heat, drain off any oil and carefully stir in the Marsala or sherry. Add the mushrooms and the meat rolls to the skillet and simmer, covered, for 15 to 20 minutes or until the veal is tender or the turkey is no longer pink, turning the rolls once during cooking. Remove the meat rolls and mushrooms to a warm platter and remove the wooden picks.

6 Bring the pan juices to boiling and boil until the juices are slightly thickened (or to the desired consistency). Spoon the juices over the meat rolls.

7 To make Rice Piedmont: In a large bowl, combine the rice, peas, butter and nutmeg. Gently fold in the Parmesan cheese being careful not to overmix the rice. Serve with the veal or turkey rolls and juices.

 TIPS FROM OUR KITCHEN

If veal scallopini isn't available, substitute ½-inch-thick pieces of veal round steak and pound them to a ⅛-inch thickness.

Nutrition Analysis (*Per Serving*): Calories: 523 / Cholesterol: 117 mg / Carbohydrates: 39 g / Protein: 39 g / Sodium: 609 mg / Fat: 21 g (Saturated Fat: 8 g) / Potassium: 669 mg.

VEAL ROLLS WITH RICE PIEDMONT

Veal Marsala

VEAL MARSALA

Makes 6 Servings

2	tablespoons cooking oil
1	clove garlic, minced
1½	pounds veal round steak, about ½ inch thick
¼	cup all-purpose flour
¼	teaspoon salt
⅛	teaspoon pepper
½	cup dry Marsala wine
¼	cup water
1	teaspoon snipped parsley
⅛	teaspoon pepper
1	4½-ounce can sliced mushrooms, drained
½	teaspoon instant chicken bouillon granules

♦   ♦   ♦

Marree Paulson told us that she created this recipe herself. After many years of eating and enjoying veal but being unable to find a good recipe, she decided to experiment with different ingredients until she found a veal recipe she enjoyed. Marree is a part-time caterer and has served Veal Marsala many times because it can be easily doubled or tripled to serve a crowd.

Marree Paulson
Taster's Choice
Stone Ridge Library
Stone Ridge
NEW YORK

1 Place the veal cutlets between 2 pieces of heavy-duty, clear plastic wrap. Pound the cutlets with the flat side of a meat mallet until the cutlets are thin and even. Remove the plastic wrap.

2 In a 10-inch skillet, heat the cooking oil. Add the garlic and cook over medium-high heat until lightly browned.

3 In a small bowl, stir together the flour, salt and the ⅛ teaspoon pepper. Dip *each* veal cutlet into the flour mixture to coat both sides. Add the veal cutlets, a few at a time, to the skillet and quickly cook them over medium-

high heat for 3 to 4 minutes or until they are browned on both sides. If necessary, add *additional* cooking oil to the skillet. Return all of the veal cutlets to the skillet.

4 Meanwhile, in another small bowl, stir together the Marsala wine, water, parsley and the ⅛ teaspoon pepper. Carefully add the Marsala mixture to the browned veal cutlets in the skillet.

5 Add the mushrooms and chicken bouillon granules to the skillet. Cover and simmer about 5 minutes or until the veal is tender, stirring occasionally to thicken the sauce. Serve immediately.

 TIPS FROM OUR KITCHEN

For a more richly flavored sauce, use 1 tablespoon of butter and 1 tablespoon of cooking oil to brown the garlic.

To make coating the veal cutlets easier, mix the flour, salt and pepper in a

plastic bag. Add the cutlets, a few at a time, and shake the bag to coat.

Veal is naturally tender so it doesn't need much cooking time. Browning only a few pieces at a time ensures that they won't toughen by overcooking.

Nutrition Analysis (*Per Serving*): Calories: 238 / Cholesterol: 92 mg / Carbohydrates: 7 g / Protein: 26 g / Sodium: 314 mg / Fat: 9 g (Saturated Fat: 2 g) / Potassium: 404 mg.

VEAL PARMIGIANA

Makes 6 Servings

1½ pounds veal leg roundsteak, cut ½ inch thick
2   eggs
½   cup fine dry plain *or* seasoned bread crumbs
½   cup grated Parmesan cheese
2   tablespoons cooking oil
1   medium onion, finely chopped
2   cloves garlic, minced
1   29-ounce can tomato sauce
1   16-ounce can whole tomatoes, undrained
¾   teaspoon dried oregano, crushed
¼   teaspoon dried thyme, crushed
8   ounces mozzarella cheese, sliced
¼   cup grated Parmesan cheese

♦   ♦   ♦

Betsy Worthington's husband loves veal parmigiana and always ordered it when they were out at restaurants. Fifteen years ago, he asked Betsy to find a recipe for it. Here is Veal Parmigiana, complete with Betsy's adaptations.

Betsy Worthington
Virginia Seasons
Junior League of Richmond
Richmond
VIRGINIA

1 Cut the veal into 6 pieces. Pound each piece between 2 sheets of plastic wrap or waxed paper to ¼-inch thickness.

2 In a small bowl, slightly beat the eggs with a fork. In a shallow bowl, combine the bread crumbs and the ½ cup Parmesan cheese.

3 Dip each piece of veal, first in the beaten egg, coating both sides, then in the bread crumb mixture, turning to coat evenly.

4 In a large skillet, brown the veal in hot oil about 1½ minutes per side or until lightly browned. Using a fork or tongs, transfer the veal to a 3-quart rectangular baking dish.

5 To make the sauce: Add the onion and garlic to the skillet and cook until the onion is tender but not brown. Carefully add the tomato sauce, *undrained* tomatoes, oregano and thyme. Simmer the sauce, uncovered, about 30 minutes or until thickened.

6 Preheat the oven to 375°. Spoon *half* the sauce over the browned veal. Sprinkle with mozzarella cheese. Spoon the remaining sauce over the cheese. Sprinkle with the ¼ cup Parmesan cheese. Bake, uncovered, in the 375° oven for 20 to 30 minutes or until bubbly.

 TIPS FROM OUR KITCHEN

You can use this same sauce and cooking method for boneless pork.

For a meatless meal, use eggplant that has been peeled and thinly sliced in place of the veal.

Nutrition Analysis *(Per Serving)*: Calories: 461 / Cholesterol: 194 mg / Carbohydrates: 23 g Protein: 45 g / Sodium: 1577 mg / Fat: 21 g (Saturated Fat: 9 g) / Potassium: 1176 mg.

VEAL PARMIGIANA

HOLIDAY HAM

HOLIDAY HAM

Makes 10 Servings
Mustard Sauce:
 ¼ cup dry English mustard
 ½ cup tarragon vinegar
 4 teaspoons dark rum
 3 eggs
 ⅓ cup sugar
 4 tablespoons unsalted butter, cut up
 ½ teaspoon salt
 Dash freshly ground pepper
Ham:
 1 4 to 6-pound boneless smoked ham
 Whole cloves
 2 tablespoons Dijon-style mustard
 1 garlic clove, crushed
 2 tablespoons plum sauce
 1 teaspoon orange juice
 ¼ cup packed brown sugar

◆   ◆   ◆

Over 350 triple-tested recipes, chosen for their emphasis on fresh ingredients and for their ease of preparation, can be found in The Junior League of Cincinnati's <u>RiverFeast: Still Celebrating Cincinnati</u>. *We thank them for including this scrumptious Holiday Ham.*

<u>*RiverFeast: Still Celebrating Cincinnati*</u>
The Junior League of Cincinnati
Cincinnati
OHIO

1 To make the Mustard Sauce: In a small bowl, place the dry mustard; add the vinegar and rum. Do not stir. Cover and let the mixture stand in the refrigerator overnight.

2 Preheat oven to 325°.

3 To prepare the ham: With a sharp knife, score the top of the entire ham.

4 Stud with the whole cloves at every intersection.

5 In a small bowl, combine the Dijon-style mustard, garlic and plum sauce. Add enough orange juice to make a syrupy mixture. Spread the mixture evenly over the top and sides of the ham.

6 Sprinkle the surface of the ham with the brown sugar. Insert a meat thermometer. Bake in the 325° oven for 1¼ to 2½ hours or until the meat thermometer reads 140°F. Let the ham stand for 10 minutes; slice.

7 Meanwhile, to complete the mustard sauce: In the top of a double boiler over simmering water, place the mustard mixture and whisk until well blended. Add the eggs, one at a time, whisking vigorously after each addition.

8 Gradually whisk in the sugar until the mixture is smooth. Beat in the butter, salt and pepper.

9 Cook and whisk about 9 minutes or until thick. Do not overcook or the eggs will curdle. Serve the sauce with the freshly baked ham.

 TIPS FROM OUR KITCHEN

Refrigerate any leftover mustard sauce up to a week. It's great served cold on ham sandwiches or with sausage links, poultry or lamb.

Nutrition Analysis (*Per Serving*): Calories: 395 / Cholesterol: 173 mg / Carbohydrates: 17 g / Protein: 41 g / Sodium: 2,388 mg / Fat: 17 g (Saturated Fat: 7 g) / Potassium: 593 mg.

PRUNE-STUFFED ROAST PORK WITH POTATOES

Makes 6 Servings

6	medium potatoes
3	tablespoons margarine *or* butter, melted
½	teaspoon paprika
1	3- to 4-pound pork loin center rib roast, backbone loosened (6 ribs)
12 to 14	pitted prunes (1 cup)
1	lemon, halved
1¼	teaspoons ground ginger
¼	teaspoon salt
¼	teaspoon pepper
3	tablespoons all-purpose flour
1	10½-ounce can beef broth
½	cup milk

◆　　◆　　◆

The San Jose Auxiliary to the Lucile Salter Packard Children's Hospital at Stanford wanted to contribute to the new children's hospital. In order to raise funds, the organization put together a cookbook, Under the Willows. All of the profits from cookbook sales were used to help buy and furnish new patient rooms.

Barbara Wortley
Under the Willows
San Jose Auxiliary to the Lucile Salter Packard Children's Hospital at Stanford
San Jose
CALIFORNIA

1 Scrub the potatoes and pat dry. Partially cut each potato into ¼-inch slices, being careful not to cut through the bottoms of the potatoes. Place each potato on a large square of foil.

2 Stir together the melted margarine or butter and the paprika. Drizzle the margarine mixture over the potatoes. Wrap the foil up around each potato and set it aside. Preheat the oven to 325°.

3 Using a long, thin knife, cut a single lengthwise pocket through the meat next to the rib bone.

4 Use your fingers or a wooden spoon handle to push the prunes into the pocket, filling it completely. Rub the lemon halves over the surface of the roast. Place the roast, bone side down, in a shallow roasting pan. Sprinkle with *1 teaspoon* of the ground ginger, the salt and pepper. Insert a meat thermometer.

5 Roast the pork in the 325° oven for 1¾ to 2½ hours or until the thermometer registers 160°. Cover loosely with foil after 1 hour. Add the potatoes during the last 1½ hours of cooking. Let the roast stand 15 minutes before carving, then slice between the ribs.

6 To make the gravy: Pour the drippings into a measuring cup, scraping the roasting pan to remove any browned bits. Skim the fat, reserving up to *2 tablespoons*. In a medium saucepan, stir together the reserved fat and enough cooking oil to equal a total of 2 tablespoons, the flour and the remaining ground ginger.

7 If necessary, add enough beef broth to the pan juices to equal 1½ cups. Add the milk and the pan juice mixture to the saucepan. Cook and stir until the gravy is thickened and bubbly. Cook and stir 1 minute more. Serve the gravy with the roast and potatoes.

 TIPS FROM OUR KITCHEN

Potatoes prepared in this way are called *Hasselback* potatoes. Some cooks recommend taping 2 wooden chopsticks or wooden spoon handles to the countertop and making cuts to the chopsticks or spoon handles. Dry bread crumbs and grated Parmesan are sometimes sprinkled over the potatoes during the last 5 minutes of baking.

Nutrition Analysis (*Per Serving*): Calories: 560 / Cholesterol: 88 mg / Carbohydrates: 65 g / Protein: 33 g / Sodium: 583 mg / Fat: 20 g (Saturated Fat: 6 g) / Potassium: 1320 mg.

PRUNE-STUFFED ROAST PORK WITH POTATOES

PORK TENDERLOIN-MUSHROOM CASSEROLE

PORK TENDERLOIN-MUSHROOM CASSEROLE

Makes 6 to 8 Servings
- 4 slices bacon
- 3 cups sliced fresh mushrooms
- 2 cups thinly sliced onions
- 2 12-ounce pork tenderloins
- ½ teaspoon salt
- ½ teaspoon pepper
- ¾ cup fine dry bread crumbs
- 1 egg, beaten
- 2 tablespoons water
- ¼ cup cooking oil
- Dash dried oregano, crushed

✦ ✦ ✦

Maria Ciesla, president of the Polish Women's Civic Club, Inc., told us that she has tried Pork Tenderloin-Mushroom Casserole and it is terrific. This recipe is part of Our Recipes, which features "old-fashioned, ethnic and specialty recipes." The cookbook is now in its fourth printing and is one of the club's five annual fundraisers. The club raises $12,000 to $20,000 each year to provide Illinois students with scholarships.

Our Recipes
Polish Women's Civic Club, Inc.
Chicago
ILLINOIS

1 Preheat the oven to 350°.

2 In a large skillet, cook the bacon until crisp. Transfer the bacon to paper towels to drain; reserve the drippings. Crumble the bacon.

3 Over medium heat, cook the mushrooms and onions in the reserved bacon drippings about 5 minutes or until the vegetables are tender. Set aside.

4 Sprinkle the pork tenderloins with the salt and pepper. Place the bread crumbs in a shallow dish. Stir together the beaten egg and water in another shallow dish.

5 Fold thin ends of tenderloin under; secure with wooden toothpicks.

 TIPS FROM OUR KITCHEN

Eight ounces of fresh whole mushrooms will yield the 3 cups of sliced mushrooms called for in this recipe.

If you don't want to cook the onion and mushrooms in the reserved bacon

6 Dip the pork tenderloins, one at a time, into the bread crumbs, then into the egg mixture, then into the bread crumbs again.

7 In another large skillet over medium heat, heat the cooking oil until it is hot. Add the coated pork tenderloins and brown on all sides. Transfer the pork tenderloins to a shallow baking dish. Sprinkle with the oregano. Spoon the mushroom-onion mixture over the tenderloins; sprinkle with the crumbled bacon.

8 Bake the pork tenderloins, uncovered, in the 350° oven about 50 minutes or until done to an internal temperature of 170°.

drippings, wipe the skillet clean. Then cook the onion and mushrooms in 2 tablespoons of cooking oil, butter or margarine.

Nutrition Analysis (*Per Serving*): Calories: 337 / Cholesterol: 120 mg / Carbohydrates: 15 g / Protein: 30 g / Sodium: 408 mg / Fat: 17 g (Saturated Fat: 4 g) / Potassium: 712 mg.

PORK CHOPS PACIFICA

Makes 6 Servings

6	1-inch thick pork chops
½	teaspoon salt
¼	teaspoon pepper
2	tablespoons olive oil
1¼	cups chicken broth
1	cup long-grain rice
1	14½-ounce can Italian tomatoes, cut up
1	cup chopped green sweet peppers
⅓	cup sliced scallions *or* green onions

◆　　◆　　◆

This recipe comes from the tiny town of Hingham in North Central Montana, which was settled in the early 1900s mainly by German and Scandinavian immigrants. Today residents of Hingham are a self-reliant community of 150 people. With the closest supermarket more than 35 miles away, Isabelle Devlin's creative one-dish dinner proves that using what's on hand can be delicious.

Isabelle Devlin
Wonderful Ideas in Farm Eating
Hingham
MONTANA

1 Preheat oven to 350°.

2 Trim any visible fat from the pork chops. Sprinkle the pork chops with the salt and pepper.

3 In a large skillet, heat the oil. Brown the pork chops, 3 at a time, for 2 to 3 minutes on each side.

4 Meanwhile, in a medium saucepan, bring the broth and rice to a boil. Stir in the tomatoes, green sweet peppers and scallions or green onions. Pour the mixture into a 13x9x2-inch baking dish.

 TIPS FROM OUR KITCHEN

Trimming the excess fat from the pork chops helps to keep the rice mixture from becoming too greasy and it also helps to reduce the total fat in the recipe.

5 Arrange the pork chops on top of the rice mixture so the chops are not touching.

6 Bake the pork chops, covered, for 1 hour and 35 minutes to 1 hour and 45 minutes, or until the chops are cooked through and the rice is tender. When testing the chops for doneness, make a small cut in one of the chops; there should be no sign of pink.

This recipe requires a long baking time so that the rice will cook completely and the pork chops will be deliciously tender.

Nutrition Analysis (*Per Serving*): Calories: 522 / Cholesterol: 128 mg / Carbohydrates: 29 g / Protein: 41 g / Sodium: 552 mg / Fat: 26 g (Saturated Fat: 8 g) / Potassium: 824 mg.

PORK CHOPS PACIFICA

SWEET-AND-SOUR PORK

SWEET-AND-SOUR PORK

1   20-ounce can pineapple chunks (juice packed)
2   carrots, peeled, halved lengthwise and cut into 1-inch lengths

Sauce:

¼   cup sugar
2½ tablespoons cornstarch
½   cup catsup
⅓   cup rice vinegar
1   tablespoon soy sauce
1   tablespoon all-purpose flour
1   tablespoon cornstarch
½   teaspoon salt
¼   teaspoon pepper
1   egg
1   pound boneless pork, cut into ¾-inch cubes

Cooking oil for frying

2   medium onions, chopped (1 cup)
1   green sweet pepper, cut into ½-inch squares (1 cup)
1   clove garlic, peeled and sliced
⅔   cucumber, unpeeled and cut into ½-inch pieces (2 cups)
6   dried shiitake mushrooms, soaked and sliced (optional)
3   cups hot cooked white *or* brown rice

♦   ♦   ♦

Connie Dosen
Another Spoonful of Love
Morning Star School
Pinellas Park
FLORIDA

1 Drain the pineapple, reserving ¾ *cup* of the juice. Set aside.

2 In a saucepan, partially cook the carrots in boiling *water* to cover for 5 minutes; drain, reserving ¾ *cup* of the cooking water (or add water, if necessary, to make ¾ cup). Set aside.

3 To make the sauce: In a 3-quart saucepan, stir together the sugar and the 2½ tablespoons cornstarch. Add the reserved water, the reserved pineapple juice, the catsup, rice vinegar and soy sauce. Cook and stir until thickened and bubbly. Cook and stir for 1 minute more; set aside.

4 In a small bowl, stir together the flour, the 1 tablespoon cornstarch, the salt and pepper. Add the egg, stirring until smooth. Add the pork cubes, stirring to coat.

5 In a heavy skillet or 4-quart Dutch oven, pour cooking oil to measure ½ inch deep. When the oil is hot, add the pork cubes, a few at a time. Cook about 2 minutes or until browned on all sides. Using a slotted spoon, remove the pork from the pan; drain on paper towels. Keep warm. Repeat until all the pork cubes are cooked.

6 Carefully add the onions, green sweet pepper and garlic to the oil in the skillet. Cook for 2 minutes. Using a slotted spoon, remove the vegetables and drain on paper towels. Repeat with the carrots, cucumber and mushrooms (if using).

7 Stir the drained vegetables and pineapple into the sauce and heat through. Stir in the pork. Serve with the rice.

 TIPS FROM OUR KITCHEN

To keep the meat cubes warm, place the drained meat on a paper towel-lined baking sheet in a 300° oven.

Dried mushrooms should be soaked for 30 minutes in enough warm water to cover them. Rinse them well and squeeze to drain thoroughly. Remove and discard the tough stems.

Nutrition Analysis (*Per Serving*): Calories: 493 / Cholesterol: 70 mg / Carbohydrates: 74 g / Protein: 17 g / Sodium: 672 mg / Fat: 16 g (Saturated Fat: 3 g) / Potassium: 655 mg.

BARBECUE BUTTERFLIED LEG OF LAMB

Makes 16 Servings
Marinade:
- 1⅓ cups olive oil
- 6 tablespoons lemon juice
- 6 tablespoons water
- 3 tablespoons snipped parsley
- 1 tablespoon finely shredded lemon peel
- 1 tablespoon sugar
- 1 tablespoon salt
- 1 tablespoon garlic powder
- 1 tablespoon dry mustard
- 1 teaspoon dried oregano, crushed
- ½ teaspoon dillweed
- ½ teaspoon pepper
- 1 bay leaf

Lamb:
- 1 6-pound leg of lamb, boned and butterflied

◆   ◆   ◆

Recently, the Yolo General Hospital Foundation helped fund a new outpatient clinic area and intensive care unit for Yolo General Hospital. Both will serve the more than 44,000 residents from throughout the county who utilize the hospital facility each year.

Dona Mast
<u>*Home Cooking From*</u>
<u>*Yolo General Hospital*</u>
Yolo General Hospital
Foundation
Woodland
CALIFORNIA

1 To make the marinade: In a medium bowl, combine the olive oil, lemon juice, water, parsley, lemon peel, sugar, salt, garlic powder, dry mustard, oregano, dillweed, pepper and bay leaf.

2 To make the lamb: Place the leg of lamb in a large bowl. Pour the marinade over the lamb. Cover and refrigerate overnight, turning several times.

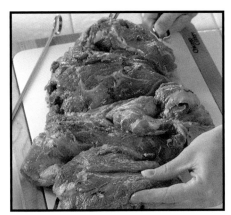

3 Drain the marinade and discard. Thread two 12- or 14-inch skewers diagonally through the lamb to keep it flat during cooking.

4 Grill the lamb over indirect medium-low heat (medium coals) for 1 to 1½ hours or until the lamb reaches the desired doneness. Add more coals as necessary. Slice thinly.

 TIPS FROM OUR KITCHEN

Save the leftovers of this roast for hearty sandwiches or a unique chef's salad.

"Fell" is a thin, parchment-like membrane that covers the fat of lamb. The fell is usually left on large cuts of lamb by the butcher. Before marinating or cooking a lamb roast, remove the fell with a sharp knife.

To bone a leg of lamb: Cut alongside the length of the bone until the surface of the bone is exposed. Work the knife around the bone to free it from the meat. Cut the meat away from one end of the bone. Lift the bone and cut away the meat from the underneath side. Carefully cut around the knobby end of the bone to completely remove the bone.

Nutrition Analysis *(Per Serving)*: Calories: 227 / Cholesterol: 86 mg / Carbohydrates: 0 g / Protein: 27 g / Sodium: 166 mg / Fat: 12 g (Saturated Fat: 3 g) / Potassium: 332 mg.

BARBECUE BUTTERFLIED LEG OF LAMB

seafood

From quick-to-the-table Simple Lemon

Sole to the more opulent Baked Fish with Rice-Olive Stuffing, this bountiful collection of seafood dishes will gladden the heart and tantalize the palate of even the fussiest fisherman in your family. Serve an enticing combination of flavors with Fillet of Sole with Bacon and Scallions or wow your family members with their own packet of Flounder in Foil. Why not tip your hat to traditional Trout Meunière, experiment with Blackened Redfish, or luxuriate in the taste and texture of Barbecued Salmon Steaks with Avocado Butter? Any recipe you hook from this chapter is sure to be the catch of the day.

STUFFED FISH MORNAY

STUFFED FISH MORNAY

Makes 4 Servings

Sauce:

3	tablespoons butter *or* margarine
¼	cup all-purpose flour
1¼	cups chicken broth
¼	cup shredded Swiss cheese
1	tablespoon grated Parmesan cheese
1	tablespoon light cream *or* half-and-half
1	teaspoon lemon juice
2	tablespoons diced, peeled tomato
⅛	teaspoon dried tarragon, crushed

Stuffing:

½	cup flaked, canned crabmeat
½	cup chopped, cooked shrimp
2	tablespoons chopped mushrooms
2	tablespoons chopped green onion
¼	teaspoon salt
¼	teaspoon dried tarragon, crushed
½	small clove garlic, minced

Fish rolls:

4	fillets of flounder, red snapper, sole *or* ocean perch (about 1 pound)
4	oysters, halved
2	tablespoons melted butter *or* margarine

Fresh tarragon (optional)

◆　　◆　　◆

Justine Halloway (Mrs. Dalton Smith) of Justine's Restaurant

1 Preheat oven to 350°. To make the sauce: Melt the butter or margarine in a saucepan over medium heat. Add the flour and whisk until smooth.

2 Cook and stir for 2 minutes. Remove from heat; stir in *1 cup* of the chicken broth.

3 Return the saucepan to the heat and stir until the mixture becomes thick and bubbly. Remove from heat and add the cheeses. At this point, reserve *¼ cup* of sauce for the stuffing.

4 Into the remaining sauce, stir the remaining chicken broth and the light cream. If necessary, add more cream to achieve the desired consistency. Stir in the lemon juice. Add the tomato and tarragon and cook over medium heat for 2 minutes. Remove from heat; keep warm.

5 To make the stuffing: Combine the ¼ cup reserved sauce with the crabmeat, shrimp, mushrooms, green onion, salt, tarragon and garlic.

6 To make the fish rolls: Spread the seafood mixture evenly over the fillets. Top with the oysters. Roll up fillets.

7 Secure the rolls with wooden toothpicks. Place in a shallow baking dish and brush with the melted butter. Bake in the 350° oven about 30 minutes or until the fish tests done. Transfer to a warm serving platter. Serve the fish with the reserved warm sauce. Garnish with fresh tarragon, if desired.

 TIPS FROM OUR KITCHEN

To make an onion-cheese sauce, omit the tomato and substitute 1 tablespoon finely chopped green onion.

Although most fish are considered relatively low in fat, some fish are still leaner than others. If you're concerned about fat, choose from the following, all of which are less than 5 percent fat: Alaska pollack, Atlantic pollack, cod, croaker, flounder, grouper, haddock, hake, halibut, ocean catfish, ocean perch, orange roughy, red snapper, sea bass, sea trout, shark, sole, swordfish and whiting. We've listed the best choices for this recipe in the ingredient list.

Nutrition Analysis (*Per Serving*): Calories: 368 / Cholesterol: 176 mg / Carbohydrates: 8 g / Protein: 37 g / Sodium: 902 mg / Fat: 20 g (Saturated Fat: 12 g) / Potassium: 577 mg.

STUFFED FISH FILLETS

   8   fresh *or* frozen fillets of sole *or* flounder
   ¼   cup margarine *or* butter
   1   stalk celery, finely chopped
   1   cup chopped fresh mushrooms
   ⅔   cup herb-seasoned stuffing mix
   1   teaspoon grated Parmesan cheese
Dash garlic powder
   1   tablespoon dry sherry
   ½   teaspoon lemon juice
   1   egg, beaten
Lemon Sauce:
   ¼   cup margarine *or* butter
   ½   cup sliced fresh mushrooms
2 to 3   teaspoons lemon juice
Dash garlic powder
   ⅛   teaspoon salt
Dash pepper
Snipped parsley

♦   ♦   ♦

The Mushroom Lover's Cookbook is a collection of recipes from the Wilmington, Delaware, branch of the American Association of University Women. Wilmington is near Kennett Square, Pennsylvania, the birthplace of mushroom growing in the United States.

The Mushroom Lover's Cookbook
The American Association of University Women, Wilmington, Delaware Branch
Wilmington
DELAWARE

1 Thaw the fish if frozen. Preheat the oven to 450°. Grease a 2-quart rectangular baking dish. Set aside.

2 To make the stuffed fish: In a medium skillet over medium heat, melt the margarine or butter. Add the celery and mushrooms and cook and stir until the vegetables are tender; remove from heat.

3 Stir in the stuffing mix, Parmesan cheese, garlic powder, dry sherry, ½ teaspoon lemon juice and beaten egg.

4 Divide the stuffing among the fillets. Wrap the ends of the fillets around the stuffing and place the rolls seam-side down in the prepared baking dish.

5 Bake, uncovered, in the 450° oven for 12 to 15 minutes or until the stuffing is hot and the fish flakes easily when tested with a fork.

6 To make the Lemon Sauce: In a small saucepan, over medium heat, melt the margarine or butter. Reduce the heat to medium-low, add the mushrooms and cook and stir for 2 minutes; remove from heat.

7 Stir in the 2 to 3 teaspoons lemon juice, garlic powder, salt and pepper. Spoon the sauce over *each* fish fillet just before serving. Sprinkle with the parsley.

 TIPS FROM OUR KITCHEN

Sole and flounder are flat saltwater fish. Both have white flesh and are delicate to mild in flavor. Authentic sole is imported from Europe. The following are varieties of flounder commonly sold in the United States: gray sole, rex sole and lemon sole (also known as winter flounder). Other varieties of flounder include sand dab (also known as American plaice) and summer flounder (also called fluke).

Use your nose when shopping for fresh fish. Check for a mild smell, not a strong odor. Fillets should appear moist and freshly cut. Fresh fish is very perishable and is best cooked the same day that it is purchased. If this isn't possible, wrap fish in moisture/vapor-proof wrap and store in the coldest part of your refrigerator up to two days.

Nutrition Analysis (*Per Serving*): Calories: 238 / Cholesterol: 61 mg / Carbohydrates: 6 g / Protein: 23 g / Sodium: 380 mg / Fat: 13 g (Saturated Fat: 3 g) / Potassium: 424 mg.

STUFFED FISH FILLETS

Baked Fish with Rice-Olive Stuffing

BAKED FISH WITH RICE-OLIVE STUFFING

Makes 8 to 10 Servings
Rice-Olive Stuffing:
- 1 cup chopped onion
- 1 cup chopped celery
- ¼ cup olive oil
- 1 cup long grain rice
- 1 16-ounce can tomatoes, cut up
- 1 cup water
- 1½ teaspoon snipped fresh mint *or* 1 tablespoon snipped fresh oregano (optional)
- 2 tablespoons snipped parsley
- 1 tablespoon snipped fresh dill
- ¼ teaspoon freshly ground pepper
- 1 cup sliced black, green *or* stuffed olives

Fish:
- 1 5- to 6-pound whole bass, cod, haddock *or* sea trout
- ½ teaspoon salt
- ¼ teaspoon freshly ground pepper
- 1 cup thinly sliced onion
- ½ cup snipped parsley
- to 1½ cups chicken broth
- 2 tablespoons cooking oil
- 2 tablespoons freshly squeezed lemon juice

◆　　◆　　◆

Popular Greek Recipes

Greek Orthodox Ladies

Philoptochos Society

Charleston

SOUTH CAROLINA

1 Grease a 1½-quart casserole dish. Set aside.

2 To make the stuffing: In a large skillet, cook and stir the onion and celery in the olive oil about 5 minutes or until tender. Add the rice, tomatoes, water, mint or oregano (if desired), parsley, dill and pepper.

3 Simmer, covered, about 25 minutes or until the rice is just tender. Stir in the olives.

4 To prepare the fish: Sprinkle the fish, inside and out, with the salt and pepper. Stuff the fish with the Rice-Olive Stuffing.

5 Preheat the oven to 500°. Meanwhile, place the onions and parsley in the prepared pan and place the stuffed fish on top. Pour in *1 cup* of the chicken broth.

6 In a small bowl, combine the cooking oil and lemon juice. Brush the fish with oil-lemon juice mixture.

7 Bake in the 500° oven for 10 minutes. Then, reduce the oven temperature to 375°; cover and bake for 30 minutes, adding more chicken stock as needed.

8 Uncover and bake about 15 minutes more or until the fish is done (fish flakes easily when tested with a fork).

 TIPS FROM OUR KITCHEN

Serving a whole fish is easy when you know the best way to remove the bones. First, position the cooked fish with the backbone toward you. Use a table knife and fork to remove the head and tail. Then make a lengthwise cut just above the backbone from the head to the tail of the fish. Next, gently loosen the top skin of the fish and peel the skin toward the stomach and away from the fish. Remove and discard the skin. Now, carefully lift the top fillet of fish away from the backbone onto a serving plate. Finally, pull up and discard the backbone and lift the bottom fillet away from the bottom skin.

Nutrition Analysis *(Per Serving)*: Calories: 339 / Cholesterol: 45 mg / Carbohydrates: 27 g / Protein: 24 g / Sodium: 496 mg / Fat: 16 g (Saturated Fat: 2 g) / Potassium: 611 mg.

FILLET OF SOLE PARMESAN

Makes 6 Servings
- ½ cup grated Parmesan cheese
- ¼ cup butter *or* margarine, softened
- 3 tablespoons mayonnaise *or* salad dressing
- 3 tablespoons chopped scallions *or* green onions

Dash bottled hot pepper sauce
- 1½ pounds skinless sole fillets *or* any fresh white fish such as orange roughy *or* red snapper
- 2 tablespoons lemon juice

Sliced scallions (optional)

◆   ◆   ◆

When the Junior League of Kansas City, Missouri, requested recipes from their 1,800 members, they received over 1,000. Then, they began the taste-testing and recipe-selection process. Each recipe was tested a minimum of three times by a committee and the recipes that passed were given to another committee who tested again for taste and presentation. Fillet of Sole Parmesan is clearly one of those that passed with flying colors!

<u>Beyond Parsley</u>
The Junior League of Kansas City
Kansas City
MISSOURI

1 Grease the rack of a broiler pan; set aside.

2 In a small bowl, stir together the Parmesan cheese, butter or margarine, mayonnaise or salad dressing, scallions or green onions and hot pepper sauce. Set aside.

3 Measure the thickness of the fish fillets, then place them in a single layer on the prepared rack of the broiler pan. Brush the fillets with the lemon juice and let stand for 10 minutes.

4 Allow 4 to 6 minutes of broiling time per ½-inch thickness of fillet. Broil the fillets 3 to 4 inches from the heat for 4 to 5 minutes. Spread the cheese mixture over the fillets. Broil for 2 to 3 minutes more or until the fish flakes easily when tested with a fork and the topping is golden. Garnish each fillet with additional sliced scallions, if desired.

 TIPS FROM OUR KITCHEN

Scallions are also called green onions. You can use as much of the green part as you want—just remove any wilted, brown or damaged tops. One green onion yields about 2 tablespoons sliced.

This buttery cheese topping is also good when spread on sliced French bread, and then broiled.

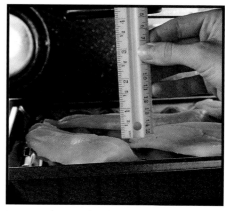

Use a ruler to check the distance from the heat source to the top of the fish—not to the top of the pan. Being too close or too far away from the heat will affect the length of broiling time.

Nutrition Analysis (*Per Serving*): Calories: 260 / Cholesterol: 92 mg / Carbohydrates: 1 g / Protein: 25 g / Sodium: 365 mg / Fat: 17 g (Saturated Fat: 8 g) / Potassium: 327 mg.

FILLET OF SOLE PARMESAN

SIMPLE LEMON SOLE

SIMPLE LEMON SOLE

Makes 4 Servings

1 pound sole fillets
1 tablespoon lemon juice
¼ cup grated Parmesan cheese
2 tablespoons margarine *or* butter, melted
4 teaspoons mayonnaise *or* salad dressing
4 teaspoons finely chopped onion (optional)
Snipped parsley (optional)
Lemon slices (optional)

◆　◆　◆

The Rodef Shalom Temple, located in Pittsburgh, Pennsylvania, is considered an historical landmark, but it was in need of extensive repairs. To raise funds, the Rodef Shalom Sisterhood created the cookbook Best of the Best. *All of the proceeds from cookbook sales were donated to their restoration fund. Recipes were contributed by members of the Sisterhood and employees of a bookstore owned by the Sisterhood.*

The Best of the Best
Rodef Shalom Sisterhood
Pittsburgh
PENNSYLVANIA

1 Grease the rack of an unheated broiler pan. Place the fish fillets on the prepared rack. Brush the fish fillets with the lemon juice and let stand for 10 minutes.

2 Broil the fish fillets 4 inches from the heat source for 4 to 6 minutes per ½-inch thickness.

3 Meanwhile, in a small bowl, stir together the Parmesan cheese, melted margarine or butter and mayonnaise or salad dressing. Add the onion, if desired.

4 When the fish fillets are almost done, spread *some* of the mayonnaise mixture over the top of *each* fillet. Broil for 2 to 3 minutes more or until the topping is golden brown. If desired, sprinkle the fish fillets with the parsley and garnish with lemon slices.

 TIPS FROM OUR KITCHEN

You can substitute fresh flounder or pike fillets for the sole in this recipe.

Properly cooked fish is opaque, begins to flake easily when tested with a fork and comes away from the bones readily. The juices should be milky white, not clear and watery.

This topping also can be used on other types of broiled fish, boneless chicken breasts or even halved baked potatoes.

For fancier lemon slices, use a stripper to remove strips of peel from the whole lemon, creating ridges. Then when you slice the lemon, these ridges will form a fancy edge around each slice.

Nutrition Analysis (*Per Serving*): Calories: 214 / Cholesterol: 61 mg / Carbohydrates: 1 g / Protein: 22 g / Sodium: 292 mg / Fat: 14 g (Saturated Fat: 3 g) / Potassium: 285 mg.

FILLET OF SOLE WITH BACON AND SCALLIONS

Makes 6 to 8 Servings

1½ to 2 pounds sole fillets
  ⅛ teaspoon salt
  ¼ teaspoon pepper
  2 tablespoons lemon juice
  ¼ teaspoon dried dillweed
  4 slices bacon, cooked, drained and crumbled
  ½ cup chopped scallions *or* green onions
  ½ cup peeled, seeded and finely chopped tomato

❖   ❖   ❖

The Junior League of Wichita has lovingly prepared The Sunflower Sampler to assist in their fund-raising efforts that benefit many community projects, including the Sedgwick County Zoo, Cowtown Museum and Heritage Square Park. Proceeds from cookbook sales have also helped Wichita to become the first city in the world to have two Ronald McDonald houses.

Sunflower Sampler
Junior League of Wichita
Wichita
KANSAS

1 Preheat broiler. Lightly grease the broiler rack.

2 Arrange the sole fillets on the prepared broiler rack, tucking under any thin portions of fish. This makes the fillets about the same thickness so they cook evenly. Sprinkle the fillets with the salt and pepper.

 TIPS FROM OUR KITCHEN

We also like this vegetable-bacon topping served over flounder or pike fillets.

For a special presentation, arrange scallion tops in a grid pattern on a white plate. Place the cooked fillets on top. Thinly slice a lemon and fan the lemon slices alongside the fish. To really impress your guests, finish the dish off with a sprig of fresh dill.

3 In a small bowl, combine the lemon juice and dillweed. Brush the lemon juice mixture evenly over the fillets.

4 In another small bowl, combine the bacon with the scallions or green onions and tomato; spoon the bacon mixture over the fillets.

5 Broil the fillets 4 to 5 inches from the heat for 3 to 5 minutes or until the fish flakes easily when tested with a fork.

Nutrition Analysis *(Per Serving):* Calories: 132 / Cholesterol: 64 mg / Carbohydrates: 1 g / Protein: 23 g / Sodium: 206 mg / Fat: 3 g (Saturated Fat: 1 g) / Potassium: 371 mg.

FILLET OF SOLE WITH BACON AND SCALLIONS

FILLET OF SOLE DUGLERE

FILLET OF SOLE DUGLERE

Makes 4 Servings
- 1 pound fresh *or* frozen skinless sole, flounder *or* other thin fish fillets, thawed

Sauce:
- 3 tablespoons butter *or* margarine
- ¼ cup finely chopped onion
- 2 tablespoons all-purpose flour
- ½ cup dry white wine
- ¼ cup water
- ½ cup whipping cream
- 3 large tomatoes, peeled and chopped
- 1 teaspoon snipped parsley
- ⅛ teaspoon dried tarragon, crushed
- ⅛ teaspoon dried dillweed
- ⅛ teaspoon dried marjoram, crushed

Topping:
- 3 tablespoons fine dry bread crumbs
- 3 tablespoons grated Parmesan cheese
- 1 tablespoon butter *or* margarine, melted

♦　♦　♦

Susan Payne told us, "I'm the kind of cook who takes the ideas from two or three recipes and puts them together to end up with something I like."

Susan Payne
Southern Accent
The Junior League of Pine Bluff
Pine Bluff
ARKANSAS

1 Preheat the oven to 350°. Grease a 3-quart rectangular baking dish.

2 Rinse the fish and pat dry with paper towels. Place the fish in a single layer in the prepared baking dish.

3 To make the sauce: In a medium saucepan, melt the 3 tablespoons butter or margarine. Add the onion; cook and stir until tender. Stir in the flour. Add the wine and water. Cook and stir until the mixture is thickened and bubbly; remove from heat.

4 Slowly stir in the whipping cream. Return the saucepan to the heat and simmer the sauce for 4 to 5 minutes, stirring occasionally.

5 Stir in the chopped tomatoes, parsley, tarragon, dillweed and marjoram. Simmer the sauce for 1 minute more. Spoon the sauce over the fish.

6 To make the topping: Stir together the bread crumbs, Parmesan cheese and the 1 tablespoon melted butter or margarine. Sprinkle the topping over the sauce.

7 Bake, uncovered, in the 350° oven for 15 to 20 minutes or until the fish flakes easily when tested with a fork.

Nutrition Analysis (*Per Serving*): Calories: 416 / Cholesterol: 136 mg / Carbohydrates: 16 g / Protein: 26 g / Sodium: 357 mg / Fat: 26 g (Saturated Fat: 15 g) / Potassium: 726 mg.

 TIPS FROM OUR KITCHEN

Serve this sauced fish with wild rice, orzo or spinach fettuccine.

To peel a fresh tomato: Use a fork or slotted spoon to plunge the tomato into boiling water about 30 seconds or just until the skin splits. Carefully remove the tomato and dip it into cold water. Use a sharp paring knife to pull off the skin.

Properly cooked fish is opaque and just beginning to flake easily when tested with a fork. If it resists flaking and is still translucent, cook a few minutes longer.

FLOUNDER IN FOIL

Makes 6 Servings

- 6   4-ounce fresh *or* frozen skinless flounder, sole *or* other fillets (about ¼ inch thick)
- 2   tablespoons cooking oil
- 2   medium onions, chopped (1 cup)
- ⅓   cup chopped green sweet pepper
- 1   tablespoon all-purpose flour
- 1   teaspoon garlic salt
- 1   teaspoon pepper
- ½   cup bottled clam juice
- ½   cup tomato juice
- 1   teaspoon Worcestershire sauce
- Dash bottled hot pepper sauce
- 1   tablespoon capers, drained

◆   ◆   ◆

The Hickory Service League of N.C., Inc. has three major fundraisers to generate money for their community service projects: the Thrift Shop, the Antique Fair and Market to Market. *The Antique Fair is a three-day event, at which the League sells homemade foods. The recipes for those foods can be found in* Market to Market.

Bess Cline
Market to Market
The Hickory Service
League of N.C., Inc.
Hickory
NORTH CAROLINA

1 Thaw the fish, if frozen.

2 In a large skillet, heat the cooking oil. Add the onions and green sweet pepper. Cook and stir until the vegetables are tender. Sprinkle the flour, garlic salt and pepper over the vegetables and stir until blended.

3 Carefully add the clam juice, tomato juice, Worcestershire sauce and hot pepper sauce. Cook and stir over medium heat until the sauce is slightly thickened and bubbly. Remove from heat; stir in the capers.

4 Preheat the oven to 350°.

5 Wash the fillets and pat dry. To assemble: Place each fillet in the center of a 12x12-inch piece of aluminum foil. Spoon sauce over each fish fillet.

6 Loosely wrap the foil around each fillet, being sure to seal well. Place the foil packets in a shallow baking pan. Bake in the 350° oven about 20 minutes or until the fish flakes easily when tested with a fork. Open the packets carefully to allow steam to escape.

 TIPS FROM OUR KITCHEN

Other fish choices that would work well in this recipe include pike, sole, whitefish and whiting.

If desired, substitute 1 cup clamato juice for the clam juice and the tomato juice.

Capers are the flower bud of the caper bush. They have a pungent, slightly bitter flavor and are usually pickled in vinegar or packed in salt.

To seal the foil packets, first fold the edges parallel to the length of the fish. Bring the edges together above the fish, fold together and down, as for a sack. Leave some space between the top of the fish and the foil. Repeat with the ends.

Serve the fish and sauce with rice, orzo, vermicelli or linguine.

Nutrition Analysis (*Per Serving*): Calories: 170 / Cholesterol: 60 mg / Carbohydrates: 6 g / Protein: 22 g / Sodium: 591 mg / Fat: 6 g (Saturated Fat: 1 g) / Potassium: 496 mg.

FLOUNDER IN FOIL

BAKED FISH WITH VEGETABLES

BAKED FISH WITH VEGETABLES

Makes 6 to 8 Servings

3	medium onions, cut up
3 or 4	medium zucchini, cut up
3	medium tomatoes
1	large green sweet pepper, halved and seeded
½	cup Italian parsley leaves
2 to 3	cloves garlic
½	teaspoon salt
¼	teaspoon pepper
¼	cup olive oil
1	15-ounce can tomato sauce
1½ to 2	pounds fresh *or* frozen fish fillets (1 to 1½-inches thick), thawed
1	lemon, thinly sliced

✦   ✦   ✦

On March 28, 1889, the Watch Hill Improvement Society was incorporated "to build up and beautify Watch Hill and to render it a still more inviting and desirable place of residence." Throughout the years, the organization has been responsible for town maintenance and theatrical extravaganzas, as well as many other projects.

Watch Hill Cooks
The Watch Hill
Improvement Society
Watch Hill
RHODE ISLAND

1 Fit a food processor work bowl with a coarse slicing disk. Slice the onions, zucchini, tomatoes and green sweet pepper, transferring them to a large mixing bowl as the work bowl gets full. *Or,* using a sharp knife, slice the vegetables by hand.

2 Replace the slicing disk with a steel knife. Add the parsley and garlic; process until chopped. *Or,* snip the parsley and mince the garlic by hand. Add the parsley mixture to the vegetables. Stir in the salt and pepper.

3 In a 12-inch skillet, heat *2 tablespoons* of the olive oil. Add the vegetable mixture; cook and stir over medium heat about 5 minutes or until the vegetables begin to soften. Carefully add the tomato sauce. Simmer, covered, for 10 minutes. Drain, reserving the liquid. Preheat the oven to 375°.

4 Coat the bottom of a 3-quart rectangular baking dish with the remaining olive oil; add the fish. Spoon the drained vegetables over and around the fish. Bake, uncovered, in the 375° oven for 35 to 40 minutes or until the fish flakes easily when tested with a fork.

5 While the fish is baking, return the reserved vegetable liquid to the skillet. Bring to a boil. Cook over medium heat about 5 minutes or until the liquid is reduced by half. Using a slotted spoon, serve the fish and vegetables. Spoon the sauce over each serving. Garnish with the lemon slices.

 TIPS FROM OUR KITCHEN

Lake trout, grouper, walleye pike, pike or bluefish (if available) work well for this recipe.

Italian parsley has larger, flatter, darker green leaves and a milder flavor than the more common curly-leaf parsley. To store, wash parsley and shake off the excess moisture. Wrap in paper towels and place in a plastic bag in the refrigerator up to 1 week.

Thaw frozen fish in the refrigerator overnight; do not thaw it at room temperature.

Nutrition Analysis (*Per Serving*): Calories: 349 / Cholesterol: 47 mg / Carbohydrates: 22 g / Protein: 32 g / Sodium: 670 mg / Fat: 16 g (Saturated Fat: 3 g) / Potassium: 1143 mg.

RED SNAPPER WITH ORANGE SAUCE

Makes 6 Servings

1 ½ pounds red snapper fillets
¼ teaspoon salt
⅛ teaspoon pepper
½ to 1 teaspoon minced garlic
1 tablespoon butter *or* margarine
1 teaspoon grated orange peel
3 tablespoons orange juice

Orange Sauce:
1 whole clove garlic
2 tablespoons butter *or* margarine
3 tablespoons orange juice
⅛ teaspoon ground ginger
2 tablespoons snipped parsley

◆   ◆   ◆

Since its founding in 1894, the Greater Kansas City Section of the National Council of Jewish Women has been actively supporting many community services. Proceeds from The Cook Book have gone to scholarship and literacy programs as well as programs for children, teens, the handicapped and the elderly.

The Cook Book
Greater Kansas City Section
of the National Council
of Jewish Women
Kansas City
MISSOURI

1 Preheat oven to 400°.

2 In a large baking pan, arrange the red snapper fillets in a single layer. Sprinkle the fillets with the salt and pepper.

3 In a small saucepan over medium heat, cook the minced garlic in the 1 tablespoon butter or margarine for 30 seconds.

4 Sprinkle the garlic-butter mixture, the grated orange peel and the 3 tablespoons of orange juice over the fillets.

5 Bake the fillets, uncovered, in the 400° oven until the fish flakes easily when tested with a fork. (Allow 4 to 6 minutes per ½-inch thickness of fish.) Transfer the fillets to a platter and keep warm.

6 Meanwhile, to make the Orange Sauce: In a small saucepan over medium heat, cook the garlic clove in the 2 tablespoons butter or margarine until the garlic begins to turn golden; remove and discard the garlic clove. Stir in the 3 tablespoons orange juice and the ginger.

7 To serve, spoon some of the sauce over each fillet. Sprinkle with the parsley.

TIPS FROM OUR KITCHEN

Be sure to choose a baking pan that's large enough to allow the fish fillets to lie flat without touching. This will help the fish to cook more evenly.

To test fish for doneness: Poke the tines of a fork into the thickest portion of the fish at a 45-degree angle. Then, gently twist the fork and pull up some of the flesh.

Undercooked fish is translucent, with clear juices. The flesh is firm and does not flake. Properly cooked fish is opaque with milky-white juices. The flesh flakes easily. Overcooked fish is opaque and dry. It flakes into tiny pieces.

Nutrition Analysis (*Per Serving*): Calories: 173 / Cholesterol: 57 mg / Carbohydrates: 2 g / Protein: 24 g / Sodium: 198 mg / Fat: 7 g (Saturated Fat: 4 g) / Potassium: 510 mg.

RED SNAPPER WITH ORANGE SAUCE

Fillet of Snapper Rome

FILLET OF SNAPPER ROME

Makes 4 Servings

4   6- to 8-ounce fresh *or* frozen red snapper fillets
5   tablespoons butter *or* margarine, divided
1   tablespoon lemon juice
Dash Worcestershire sauce
8   green sweet pepper strips (about ⅓ of a medium)
1   tablespoon all-purpose flour
½   cup half-and-half *or* light cream
1   6-ounce can crabmeat, drained, flaked and cartilage removed
Dash white pepper
½   cup fine dry bread crumbs

❖   ❖   ❖

A Heritage of Good Tastes has sold almost 40,000 copies, generating nearly $11,000 per year for the TWIG (originally named for the branch of the Auxiliary comprised of the youngest members). Included recipes—all triple taste-tested—were contributed by members of the TWIG and restaurants in Old Town, Alexandria.

Mrs. Ronald E. McKeown
A Heritage of Good Tastes
The TWIG, The Junior Auxiliary of the Alexandria Hospital
Alexandria
VIRGINIA

1 Thaw the fish, if frozen. Skin, if desired. Measure the thickness of the fillets. Place the fillets in a broiler pan, turning under thin edges to make an even thickness.

2 In a small saucepan, stir together *2 tablespoons* of the butter or margarine, the lemon juice and Worcestershire sauce. Cook and stir until the butter or margarine melts.

3 Broil the fish 3 to 4 inches from the heat for 4 to 6 minutes per ½-inch thickness, basting occasionally with the lemon-butter mixture. Add the green sweet pepper strips to the pan during the last 2 minutes of broiling.

4 In a medium saucepan, melt *1 tablespoon* of the butter or margarine. Stir in the flour. Stir in the half-and-half or light cream. Cook over medium heat until the mixture is thickened and bubbly, stirring constantly. Add the crabmeat and white pepper.

5 Spoon the sauce over the fish fillets.

6 Melt the remaining *2 tablespoons* of the butter or margarine. Stir in the bread crumbs. Arrange 2 green sweet pepper strips on the top of each fillet. Sprinkle with the bread crumb mixture.

7 Broil for 1 to 2 minutes more or just until the bread crumbs are browned.

 TIPS FROM OUR KITCHEN

Measuring the thickness of the fish helps to estimate the proper broiling time.

If red snapper isn't available, use lake trout, rockfish or white fish.

You can substitute red or yellow sweet peppers for the green sweet peppers.

Milk can be used instead of the half-and-half or light cream.

Nutrition Analysis (*Per Serving*): Calories: 379 / Cholesterol: 128 mg / Carbohydrates: 13 g / Protein: 35 g / Sodium: 487 mg / Fat: 20 g (Saturated Fat: 11 g) / Potassium: 713 mg.

BLACKENED REDFISH

Makes 3 Servings

- 1 tablespoon paprika
- 1 teaspoon salt
- 1 teaspoon onion powder
- 1 teaspoon garlic powder
- 1 teaspoon ground red pepper
- ¾ teaspoon white pepper
- ¾ teaspoon black pepper
- ½ teaspoon dried oregano, crushed
- ½ teaspoon dried thyme, crushed
- ¼ cup margarine *or* butter
- 3 redfish fillets, ¾ inch thick (12 ounces)

❖　❖　❖

Debbie Espy first tasted Blackened Redfish at a dinner given by a friend about five years ago. Debbie got the recipe, and when her friend came to her home for dinner, it was Debbie's turn to serve the delicious fish dish! It's very easy to make—"Cook, flip, cook and it's done!" Debbie suggests serving the redfish with steamed vegetables and French bread.

Debbie Espy
Our Daily Bread
Mountain View Baptist Church
Stone Mountain
GEORGIA

1 In a small dish, stir together the paprika, salt, onion powder, garlic powder, red pepper, white pepper, black pepper, oregano and thyme; set aside.

2 Melt the margarine or butter. Dip the fish in the margarine or butter, then sprinkle each side with about *1 teaspoon* of the spice mixture. Place the coated fish in single layer on a platter.

3 Outdoors, on a camping stove or a grill, heat an ungreased 10-inch cast-iron skillet directly on the hot coals until it is very hot; keep hot. Carefully place the coated fish in the skillet and cook approximately 2 minutes on each side or until the fish flakes when tested with a fork. Each side will look black. Serve immediately.

 TIPS FROM OUR KITCHEN

Because a great deal of smoke is given off when you blacken fish, cooking outdoors is highly recommended.

To prepare the fish on a grill: Remove the grill rack and heat the coals until hot. Set an ungreased cast-iron skillet directly on the coals and heat for 5 minutes or until a drop of water sizzles when dropped in the skillet. Add the coated fish and cook about 2 minutes on each side.

Store any remaining spice mixture in a covered container.

Redfish is a saltwater fish with firm, white meat and a mild flavor; it is sometimes called red drum. Because so much was taken from the Gulf of Mexico in the 1980s, authorities banned the commercial redfish harvest. Black drum is a good substitute. This cooking method also works well with other types of fish such as croaker, carp, cod or haddock.

Cajun cooking is the cuisine of French-speaking south Louisiana. It features simple, one-pot dishes with French, Italian, Spanish, African, Indian and southern influences. The name *cajun* comes from *Acadian*, the name for the early French-Canadian settlers.

Nutrition Analysis (*Per Serving*): Calories: 261 / Cholesterol: 42 mg / Carbohydrates: 3 g / Protein: 24 g / Sodium: 704 mg / Fat: 17 g (Saturated Fat: 3 g) / Potassium: 531 mg.

Blackened Redfish

Fried Halibut Steaks with Hot Tartar Sauce

Fried Halibut Steaks with Hot Tartar Sauce

Makes 6 Servings
- 2 pounds halibut steak, cut ¾- to 1-inch thick
- ¾ cup fine dry bread crumbs
- ½ teaspoon seasoned salt
- 3 tablespoons butter *or* margarine
- 2 tablespoons fresh lemon juice

Hot Tartar Sauce:
- 1 tablespoon butter *or* margarine
- 1 teaspoon all-purpose flour
- ½ cup milk
- ⅓ cup mayonnaise *or* salad dressing
- 1 to 2 tablespoons chopped dill pickle
- 1 tablespoon chopped onion
- 2 teaspoons snipped parsley

◆ ◆ ◆

Georgeann Gaston enjoys cooking, but she likes simple dishes because she does not enjoy spending the entire day in the kitchen preparing a meal. That's why this recipe for Fried Halibut Steaks with Hot Tartar Sauce is the perfect recipe for her. Her family loves it, too, particularly because it isn't heavily spiced.

Georgeann Gaston
<u>Cabaret Cuisine</u>
The Longview Junior Service League
Longview
WASHINGTON

1 Cut the halibut steak into 6 portions. Rinse the fish steaks and pat dry with paper towels.

2 In a shallow dish, stir together the bread crumbs and seasoned salt. Coat *each* fish steak with the bread crumb mixture.

3 In a large skillet, melt the 3 tablespoons butter or margarine; stir in the lemon juice. Place the fish steaks in a single layer in the hot lemon butter.

4 Fry over medium heat for 7 to 9 minutes or until the fish flakes easily when tested with a fork, turning the steaks once halfway through cooking.

5 Using a spatula, carefully transfer the fish steaks to paper towels to drain; keep the fish warm.

6 To make the Hot Tartar Sauce: In a small saucepan, melt the 1 tablespoon butter or margarine. Stir in the flour. Add the milk all at once to the flour mixture. Cook and stir over medium heat until the mixture is thickened and bubbly. Cook and stir for 1 minute more. Stir in the mayonnaise or salad dressing, dill pickle, onion and parsley. Heat the sauce through.

7 Place the Fried Halibut Steaks on a serving platter. Pour the Hot Tartar Sauce over the fish steaks. Or, serve the Hot Tartar Sauce on the side and garnish with lemon slices and fresh dill, if desired.

 Tips from Our Kitchen

Halibut steaks are sold fresh and frozen. If you're using frozen steaks, thaw them in the refrigerator according to the package directions before coating and frying them.

You'll need a 10- to 12-inch skillet to fit the 2 pounds of halibut steaks in a single layer.

The bread crumb coating and lemon butter would also be good with salmon steaks.

For a sweeter tartar sauce, substitute pickle relish or chopped sweet pickle for the dill pickle.

Nutrition Analysis (*Per Serving*): Calories: 388 / Cholesterol: 78 mg / Carbohydrates: 12 g / Protein: 34 g / Sodium: 458 mg / Fat: 22 g (Saturated Fat: 7 g) / Potassium: 751 mg.

TROUT MEUNIÈRE

Makes 6 Servings

6	dressed trout or 6 freshwater bass fillets
½	cup fine saltine cracker crumbs (15 crackers)
¼	cup butter *or* margarine
1	2-ounce package slivered almonds
½	cup dry white wine
2	tablespoons lemon juice
2	tablespoons snipped parsley

Lemon twists (optional)
Parsley sprigs (optional)

◆ ◆ ◆

Hearts & Flours is now in its third printing, continuing to fulfill its purpose of funding special projects of the Junior League of Waco, Texas. The League is known for its innovative and effective volunteer programs, and its current focus is on the city's youth. Proceeds from cookbook sales will help to fund programs aimed at reducing teenage pregnancy and encouraging high school graduation, among others.

Hearts & Flours
Junior League of Waco
Waco
TEXAS

1 Rinse the fish; do not pat dry. Roll each piece of fish in the cracker crumbs.

2 In a large skillet, melt *2 tablespoons* of the butter or margarine. Add the fish pieces and gently cook for 2 to 3 minutes on each side or until the fish flakes when tested with a fork. Do not overcook.

3 Using a spatula, carefully remove the fish from the skillet and transfer to a serving platter. Keep warm.

4 Melt the remaining 2 tablespoons butter in the skillet. Add the almonds and cook and stir until the almonds are lightly browned. Spoon the almonds over the fish.

5 Add the wine, lemon juice and snipped parsley to the skillet. Simmer for 2 minutes. Pour the sauce over the fish and almonds.

6 Garnish the fish with the lemon twists and the parsley sprigs, if desired.

 TIPS FROM OUR KITCHEN

If you're watching your sodium intake, use low-sodium saltine crackers.

For added flavor, add a pinch of fresh or dried herbs to the cracker crumbs. Basil, dillweed or savory would work well with the flavor from the almonds.

Here's how to make sure the fish you buy is fresh. First, use your nose. Fresh fish in any form has a fresh, mild odor.

Next, take a good look. For whole, drawn or dressed fish, look for shiny, taut and iridescent skin and clear, bright eyes. The gills should be bright red or pink and not slippery.

Fillets should have a moist appearance with clean cuts. Ragged edges and discoloration indicate poor quality.

Buy equal-sized fish or pieces of fish to ensure uniform doneness.

Nutrition Analysis *(Per Serving)*: Calories: 433 / Cholesterol: 152 mg / Carbohydrates: 7 g / Protein: 49 g / Sodium: 234 mg / Fat: 21 g (Saturated Fat: 7 g) / Potassium: 1228 mg.

TROUT MEUNIÈRE

DOC'S SALMON

DOC'S SALMON

Makes 4 Servings

4	salmon fillets, 4 to 6 ounces each
2	tablespoons butter *or* margarine, melted
2	teaspoons soy sauce
2	teaspoons lemon juice
1	tablespoon snipped fresh chives
1	tablespoon snipped parsley
¼	teaspoon garlic powder
¼	teaspoon onion powder
⅛	teaspoon pepper

✦ ✦ ✦

Dr. F.J. (Doc) Donahue is a retired dentist and self-proclaimed "Northwestern man." From an area where fresh fish is abundant, Doc created this method for preparing salmon as an alternative to the common method of cooking it with barbecue sauce. Everyone enjoys the dish, especially Doc's daughter, Jo Beck, who says that she serves the dish often.

Dr. F.J. Donahue
Cabaret Cuisine
Longview Junior Service League
Longview
WASHINGTON

1 Preheat oven to 350°. Create a "baking pan" from a piece of heavy-duty foil by folding up approximately 1 inch on all sides and crimping the corners. Place the foil on an ungreased baking pan or cookie sheet.

2 Place the salmon fillets on the foil. Cut 6 or 7 slashes in each fillet to allow for better penetration of seasonings.

3 In a small bowl, combine the melted butter or margarine, soy sauce, lemon juice, chives, parsley, garlic powder, onion powder and pepper.

4 Brush the butter mixture on the salmon fillets.

5 Bake, uncovered, in the 350° oven for 15 to 20 minutes or until the fish flakes easily when tested with a fork.

 TIPS FROM OUR KITCHEN

Try this flavorful butter mixture brushed on cod, haddock or other white fish fillets, too.

Use the baking foil to wrap any leftover fish.

Leftover salmon is a versatile addition to many dishes. Add leftover salmon to a creamed soup for a tasty change. Flake it on a lettuce salad to add color and food value, or use the cooked salmon in place of chicken or tuna in your favorite salad recipes.

Nutrition Analysis *(Per Serving)*: Calories: 240 / Cholesterol: 36 mg / Carbohydrates: 18 g / Protein: 22 g / Sodium: 395 mg / Fat: 11 g (Saturated Fat: 5 g) / Potassium: 1509 mg.

Fresh Salmon with Vegetables

1 Preheat the oven to 450°.

2 Cut the parchment paper into *six* 16x12-inch pieces. Place *1* bay leaf in the center of *each* piece of parchment paper; set aside.

3 Sprinkle the salmon steaks with the salt and pepper; set aside.

4 Divide the carrots, celery, leeks, mushrooms and shallots in half; toss together. Evenly sprinkle the tossed vegetables from 1 bowl over *each* piece of parchment paper. Place *1* piece of salmon on top of the vegetables. Toss together the remaining vegetables. Evenly sprinkle the vegetables over each piece of salmon.

5 Bring 2 opposite edges of each piece of parchment paper together and pleat to form a seal. Fold over the ends to make a neat bundle. The fish should be wrapped tightly in the paper. Arrange the bundles, seam side down, on a baking sheet. Bake in the 450° oven for 15 to 20 minutes or until the fish flakes easily when tested with a fork; *do not overcook.*

6 Remove the bundles from the oven and place them on dinner plates. Cut the paper down the center and remove the bay leaves. Serve the fish on the paper and garnish with the lemon wedges.

 Tips from Our Kitchen

Placing the bay leaves directly on the parchment paper means that they will be on top when you remove them before serving.

It's best to use a skinless salmon fillet because if you substitute a salmon steak with the skin still on, the oil from the skin will be trapped in the parchment paper.

If you like your vegetables more than crisp-tender, you may want to cook them in boiling water for 1 to 2 minutes before adding them to the packets.

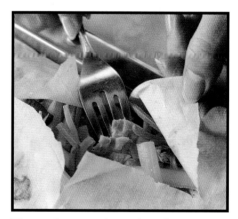

To avoid overcooking the salmon, check for doneness after 15 minutes. To check for doneness, slit the wrapping in one of the packages near the middle of the oven and use a fork to test if the salmon flakes easily.

Nutrition Analysis (*Per Serving*): Calories: 216 / Cholesterol: 31 mg / Carbohydrates: 14 g / Protein: 26 g / Sodium: 261 mg / Fat: 6 g (Saturated Fat: 1 g) / Potassium: 625 mg.

FRESH SALMON WITH VEGETABLES

POACHED FISH WITH DILL SAUCE

POACHED FISH WITH DILL SAUCE

Makes 6 Servings

 6   salmon *or* other fish steaks,
     cut 1 inch thick (about 2
     pounds total)
 ½   teaspoon salt
 ¼   teaspoon whole black peppers
 ½   cup dry white wine
 ¼   cup lemon juice
 2   bay leaves

Dill Sauce:
 2   tablespoons butter *or*
     margarine
 1   tablespoon chopped green
     onion
 1   tablespoon all-purpose flour
 1   cup half-and-half *or* light
     cream
 ½   teaspoon salt
 ¼   teaspoon dried dillweed
Dash white pepper
 2   tablespoons chopped
     pimiento
 1   tablespoon lemon juice
 2   teaspoons prepared mustard

✦   ✦   ✦

*Betty Di Masi and her husband
really enjoy cooking and have
collected numerous fish recipes
over the years. Mr. Di Masi said
that their favorite poaching
method is to add a little cumin
powder and lime juice to the water.*

Betty Di Masi
Around the World, Around Our
Town: Recipes from San Pedro
Friends of the San Pedro Library
San Pedro
CALIFORNIA

1 Place the fish steaks in a large skillet and sprinkle with the ½ teaspoon salt and the black peppers. Add the white wine, the ¼ cup lemon juice, the bay leaves and enough *water* to cover the fish steaks.

2 Bring the wine mixture to a boil; reduce heat. Cover and simmer for 8 to 12 minutes or until the fish flakes easily when tested with a fork.

3 Meanwhile, to make the Dill Sauce: In a small saucepan, melt the butter or margarine. Add the green onion and cook just until soft. Stir in the flour.

4 Add the half-and-half or light cream, the ½ teaspoon salt, the dillweed and white pepper to the flour mixture. Cook and stir over medium heat until the mixture is thickened and bubbly; cook and stir for 1 minute more. Add the pimiento, the 1 tablespoon lemon juice and the mustard. Stir until the sauce is smooth and well blended.

5 Using a metal spatula, transfer the fish steaks to a heated serving platter. Spoon the Dill Sauce over the fish steaks and serve.

 TIPS FROM OUR KITCHEN

You can substitute swordfish, tuna, bluefish or sea bass for the salmon in this recipe.

If you want to use fresh lemon juice in this recipe, you'll need 2 medium lemons. To get the most juice, bring the lemons to room temperature and then roll them under your palm against the kitchen counter before squeezing them.

You might prefer to substitute a flavored mustard, such as horseradish mustard or Dijon-style mustard, for the plain prepared mustard in the sauce.

Poaching is a great no-fat cooking method. Just be sure to keep the cooking liquid at a simmer—not a boil—so the fish doesn't overcook.

Nutrition Analysis (*Per Serving*): Calories: 248 / Cholesterol: 52 mg / Carbohydrates: 4 g / Protein: 23 g / Sodium: 525 mg / Fat: 14 g (Saturated Fat: 6 g) / Potassium: 305 mg.

BARBECUED SALMON STEAKS WITH AVOCADO BUTTER

Makes 6 Servings

6 salmon steaks, cut 1 inch thick (about 3 pounds)

Marinade:
½ cup cooking oil
3 tablespoons lemon juice
2 teaspoons barbecue spice
¼ teaspoon dried basil, crushed
¼ teaspoon dried marjoram, crushed
¼ teaspoon pepper
Dash salt

Avocado Butter:
½ cup butter *or* margarine, softened
¼ cup mashed avocado
4 teaspoons lemon juice
1 tablespoon snipped parsley
1 teaspoon Worcestershire sauce
¼ teaspoon garlic salt
Parsley sprigs (optional)
Lemon slices (optional)

✦ ✦ ✦

Over thirty-five years ago, Jo-Anne Brown received this recipe from a cook on a yacht in California. Although she has altered the recipe over the years, one ingredient—the avocado—has endured. Jo-Anne says emphatically, "The more avocado, the better."

Jo-Anne Brown
Mark Twain Library Cookbook
The Mark Twain Library
Association
Redding
CONNECTICUT

1 Thaw the salmon steaks, if frozen. Place the fish steaks in a single layer in a 13x9x2-inch baking dish.

2 To make the marinade: In a glass jar with a tight-fitting lid, combine the cooking oil, the 3 tablespoons lemon juice, the barbecue spice, basil, marjoram, pepper and salt. Shake well and pour the marinade over the salmon. Cover and refrigerate for 1 hour, turning the fish once.

3 To make the Avocado Butter: In a blender container or food processor bowl, blend or process the butter or margarine, avocado, the 4 teaspoons lemon juice, the snipped parsley, Worcestershire sauce and garlic salt until smooth. Refrigerate the mixture in a covered container until ready to serve.

4 Drain the fish, reserving the marinade. Place the fish on a greased grill rack. Grill, uncovered, directly over medium-hot coals for 5 minutes. Using a wide spatula, carefully turn the fish over and brush with the reserved marinade. Grill for 3 to 7 minutes more or until the fish flakes easily when tested with a fork. Arrange the fish on a serving platter. Dollop each fish steak with Avocado Butter. Garnish with parsley sprigs and lemon slices, if desired.

 TIPS FROM OUR KITCHEN

Try swordfish or halibut steaks in place of the salmon.

You'll need 2 lemons for this recipe. Use 1½ lemons for the juice and the remaining for the optional slices.

One hour is long enough for marinating fish when the marinade contains an acid such as lemon juice. Marinating any longer will toughen the fish.

To broil the fish: Grease the rack of a broiler pan. Drain the fish, reserving the marinade. Place the fish on the prepared broiler rack and broil 4 inches from the heat for 5 minutes. Using a wide spatula, carefully turn the fish over and brush with the reserved marinade. Broil for 3 to 7 minutes more or until the fish flakes easily when tested with a fork.

Nutrition Analysis (*Per Serving*): Calories: 402 / Cholesterol: 82 mg / Carbohydrates: 1 g / Protein: 33 g / Sodium: 521 mg / Fat: 29 g (Saturated Fat: 12 g) / Potassium: 389 mg.

BARBECUED SALMON STEAKS WITH AVOCADO BUTTER

SHRIMP SCAMPI

SHRIMP SCAMPI

Makes 4 Servings

1½	pounds fresh large shrimp (about 24)
½	cup butter *or* margarine
¼	cup snipped parsley
½	teaspoon salt
¼	teaspoon freshly cracked pepper
2	cloves garlic, minced
1	cup dry white wine
1	tablespoon lemon juice
1	tablespoon all-purpose flour

Parsley

◆　　◆　　◆

The Junior Service League of Killeen, Inc. spent two years creating Central Texas Style. *In addition to the recipes, there are original pen and ink sketches by a native Texan artist on each divider page, as well as a local artist's painting of the landscape in central Texas on the cover of the book. The attractive appearance and the simplicity of the cookbook are the highlights of* Central Texas Style.

Mary Ann Shearer Gray
Central Texas Style
Junior Service League
of Killeen, Inc.
Killeen
TEXAS

1 Shell and devein the shrimp. In a large skillet over medium heat, melt ¼ *cup* of the butter or margarine. Add the shrimp to the skillet and cook and stir for 3 to 5 minutes or until the shrimp are opaque. Transfer the shrimp to a bowl; set aside.

2 Melt the remaining butter or margarine in the skillet. Add the ¼ cup parsley, the salt, pepper and garlic. Cook the mixture for 1 minute. Stir in the white wine and lemon juice. Cook for 4 to 5 minutes or until the mixture is reduced to *¾ cup.*

3 Add the flour to the wine mixture, whisking until the mixture is combined. Continue to cook and stir until the sauce is thickened and bubbly.

4 Return the shrimp to the skillet and cook until the shrimp are heated through. Garnish with the additional parsley.

 TIPS FROM OUR KITCHEN

After shelling and deveining, 24 large shrimp yield about 1 pound of shrimp for cooking.

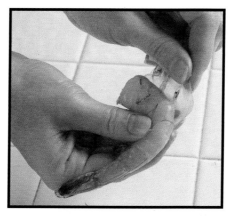

To remove the shell from a shrimp: Carefully make a shallow cut lengthwise down the body, cutting just through the shell. Hold the shrimp in one hand; starting at the head end, carefully peel the shell back and away from the shrimp. Leave the last section

of the shell and tail intact. Gently pull on the tail portion to remove the entire shell.

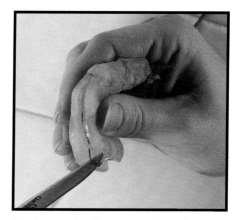

To devein the shrimp: Make a shallow slit with a sharp knife along the back of the shrimp. Use the tip of the knife to scrape out the black vein.

If desired, substitute chicken broth for all or part of the wine in this recipe.

Nutrition Analysis (*Per Serving*): Calories: 350 / Cholesterol: 257 mg / Carbohydrates: 3 g / Protein: 22 g / Sodium: 728 mg / Fat: 24 g (Saturated Fat: 14 g) / Potassium: 272 mg.

EASTERN SHORE CRABCAKES

Makes 4 to 6 Servings

¼	cup butter *or* margarine
1	medium onion, chopped
¼	cup snipped parsley
½	cup all-purpose flour
1	cup milk
2	eggs
12 to 16	ounces fresh, frozen *or* canned cooked crabmeat, thawed, if frozen
¼	teaspoon salt
⅛	teaspoon pepper
1	cup cracker crumbs
3	eggs, beaten
¼	cup cooking oil

❖ ❖ ❖

Mary Bushey says that she reads her collection of cookbooks from her friends from all over the country like others read novels. This recipe, she reports, came to her from a "little grandmother" in Maryland. She sometimes makes Eastern Shore Crabcakes as hors d'oeuvres by forming the mixture into smaller cakes.

Mary W. Bushey
Critics' Choice
The Guild of Corinth
Theatre Arts
Corinth
MISSISSIPPI

1 In a large skillet, melt the butter or margarine. Add the onion and parsley and cook until the onion is tender. Add the flour and stir until blended.

2 In a small bowl, beat together the milk and 2 eggs; add to the hot mixture. Cook, stirring constantly, until the mixture is thick and coming away from the sides of the pan.

3 Add the crabmeat and mix well. Season with the salt and pepper. Cool.

4 Form the mixture into 8 to 12 flat cakes ½ to ¾-inch thick. Dip the cakes into the 3 beaten eggs and then roll in cracker crumbs.

 TIPS FROM OUR KITCHEN

The crab mixture is easier to form into even patties if you let it cool slightly before shaping. Moistening your hands before you shape each patty helps, too.

5 In a large skillet, fry the crabcakes in hot oil over medium heat about 2 minutes per side or until golden brown. Using a slotted spatula, remove the crabcakes from the pan and drain on paper towels.

Nutrition Analysis (*Per Serving*): Calories: 580 / Cholesterol: 392 mg / Carbohydrates: 31 g / Protein: 29 g / Sodium: 1045 mg / Fat: 3 g (Saturated Fat: 13 g) / Potassium: 356 mg.

EASTERN SHORE CRABCAKES

recipe index

Metric Cooking Hints

By making a few conversions, cooks in Australia, Canada, and the United Kingdom can use the recipes in *America's Best-Loved Community Cookbook Recipes: Family Dinners* with confidence. The charts on this page provide a guide for converting measurements from the U.S. customary system, which is used throughout this book, to the imperial and metric systems. There also is a conversion table for oven temperatures to accommodate the differences in oven calibrations.

Volume and Weight: Americans traditionally use cup measures for liquid and solid ingredients. The chart (top right) shows the approximate imperial and metric equivalents. If you are accustomed to weighing solid ingredients, here are some helpful approximate equivalents.

■ 1 cup butter, caster sugar, or rice = 8 ounces = about 250 grams
■ 1 cup flour = 4 ounces = about 125 grams
■ 1 cup icing sugar = 5 ounces = about 150 grams
  Spoon measures are used for smaller amounts of ingredients. Although the size of the tablespoon varies slightly among countries. However, for practical purposes and for recipes in this book, a straight substitution is all that's necessary.
  Measurements made using cups or spoons should always be level, unless stated otherwise.

Product Differences: Most of the ingredients called for in the recipes in this book are available in English-speaking countries. However, some are known by different names. Here are some common American ingredients and their possible counterparts:
■ Sugar is granulated or caster sugar.
■ Powdered sugar is icing sugar.
■ All-purpose flour is plain household flour or white flour. When self-rising flour is used in place of all-purpose flour in a recipe that calls for leavening, omit the leavening agent (baking soda or baking powder) and salt.
■ Light corn syrup is golden syrup.
■ Cornstarch is cornflour.
■ Baking soda is bicarbonate of soda.
■ Vanilla is vanilla essence.

Useful Equivalents

⅛ teaspoon = 0.5ml
¼ teaspoon = 1ml
½ teaspoon = 2 ml
1 teaspoon = 5 ml
¼ cup = 2 fluid ounces = 50ml
⅓ cup = 3 fluid ounces = 75ml
½ cup = 4 fluid ounces = 125ml
⅔ cup = 5 fluid ounces = 150ml
¾ cup = 6 fluid ounces = 175ml
1 cup = 8 fluid ounces = 250ml
2 cups = 1 pint
2 pints = 1 litre
½ inch =1 centimetre
1 inch = 2 centimetres

Baking Pan Sizes

American	Metric
8x1½-inch round baking pan	20x4-centimetre sandwich or cake tin
9x1½-inch round baking pan	23x3.5-centimetre sandwich or cake tin
11x7x1½-inch baking pan	28x18x4-centimetre baking pan
13x9x2-inch baking pan	32.5x23x5-centimetre baking pan
12x7½x2-inch baking dish	30x19x5-centimetre baking pan
15x10x2-inch baking pan	38x25.5x2.5-centimetre baking pan (Swiss roll tin)
9-inch pie plate	22x4- or 23x4-centimetre pie plate
7- or 8-inch springform pan	18- or 20-centimetre springform or loose-bottom cake tin
9x5x3-inch loaf pan	23x13x6-centimetre or 2 pound narrow loaf pan or paté tin
1½-quart casserole	1.5-litre casserole
2-quart casserole	2-litre casserole

Oven Temperature Equivalents

Farenheit Setting	Celsius Setting*	Gas Setting
300°F	150°C	Gas Mark 2
325°F	160°C	Gas Mark 3
350°F	180°C	Gas Mark 4
375°F	190°C	Gas Mark 5
400°F	200°C	Gas Mark 6
425°F	220°C	Gas Mark 7
450°F	230°C	Gas Mark 8
Broil		Grill

Electric and gas ovens may be calibrated using Celsius. However, increase the Celsius setting 10 to 20 degrees when cooking above 160°C with an electric oven. For convection or forced-air ovens (gas or electric), lower the temperature setting 10°C when cooking at all heat levels.